Memoirs of an
Ordinary Guy

To everyone, everywhere, we all have a story.

Author: E. J. Rosenwinkel

Dedication

To everyone, everywhere, my hope is that you find a piece of yourself within these chapters. Throughout the chaos and uncertainty of life, remember to keep your eyes and mind open and be willing to learn and grow. We are all unique and have a story that we can share.

Acknowledgment

To the people that I have met along the way, from across the Americas, Europe, Mexico, Asia, Africa and the Middle East, you have touched my life and influenced how I see the world today. To my children and entire family, thank you for being part of this journey, as crazy as it may be.

Contents

Prelude

Life is a wild ride, isn't it? A rollercoaster of experiences and memories that shape how we see the world and interact with those around us. Some of these moments are routine, others hilarious, some deep and painful, and then there are those so unbelievably crazy, you'd think they were straight out of a movie.

Life's not a rehearsal, it's your moment, right here, right now, on this stage. Don't hold back. Embrace every twist, every turn, every wild curve it throws your way. Whether you're at the peak of success or navigating through life's challenges, seize it all. Tomorrow isn't guaranteed, so why wait?

Let's face it: life's full of surprises. It's a blend of highs and lows, victories and setbacks. Amidst the distractions and drama that threaten to derail us, staying focused on our personal growth and journey is key.

I'm not a celebrity, not a superstar athlete or a public figure, just an ordinary guy. But let me share with you, my story. It's a tale filled with the bizarre, the heart-pounding, and the downright unbelievable. It's real, it's raw, and it's my journey, a journey that's taught me more than I ever imagined.

So, buckle up. Here's to embracing the unexpected, learning from the chaos, and living every moment like it's the only one that matters. This is my life, laid bare and unfiltered.

Chapter 1
Shoot for the Stars or Go Under the Bridge

It was a scorching summer in the upper Midwest, the days stretching long into June. School's spring break had freed me and my two closest buddies, and as the fourth of July approached, we brainstormed for things to do to fill the hours. Lounging in the park, riverside, with other kids buzzing about their summer plans, we were determined to top them all with an epic tale.

Back in those days, summer was all about freedom

and mischief. We'd roll out of our houses in the morning on our sleek Schwinn or Raleigh banana bikes, cruising through the streets with our crew. Our destination? The river, our playground of endless adventure.

We'd spend the days soaking up the sun, diving into the cool waters, hiking the rugged trails like we owned them. And, of course, we strutted our stuff, trying to impress the girls from our town. Every moment was charged with the thrill of possibility, the air thick with laughter and the promise of youthful indiscretions.

It was like "Groundhog day" all summer, ending each day by heading home at night, then cleaning up in preparation for the traditional family dinner. If lucky enough, after dinner, on occasion, our parents would grant one of us the use of the family car to hit the streets and venture to the local Dairy Queen, a treat all unto itself. We were fortunate that my one friend, the local rich kid, had his own car, so he would do the driving when none of us could succeed at getting the keys for the family cruiser. While we looked forward to the vanilla swirl cones and Mister Misty floats, our real choice of dessert was to hook up with the local girls from our class. Our dilemma: in order to support our ice cream habits and an opportunity for romance with one of these sweetheart beauties, we needed cash.

As the summer days progressed, soon approaching July, with pencil and notebook in hand, we started to write down every idea we could think of to make some money. As we lounged by the banks of the river and after a few hours or so of collecting our thoughts, our list grew with a number of options: washing cars, cleaning garages, cutting grass, babysitting (though at that time in life, this was a role reserved for girls and I already had a younger brother I had to watch over anyway), helping to find lost cats and dogs, dishwashing, and the list went on and on.

My rich kid friend, the one with his own car didn't add much to the list as he seemed to always have money lining his pockets. What he did offer, however, was an older sibling that had just earned his multi-engine pilot's license, making him the ultimate "pilot in command." Then it hit us like a fireworks finale, literally fireworks! We'd buy them in South Dakota and sell them where they weren't available, in our hometown and state. After a day of discussion with his older brother, who knew of a place to buy the goods and also liked the idea, I think due more to the thrill of it all, we were set to go. Our ride? A sleek Cessna 310, six seats and dual engines, piloted by our rich friend's daredevil brother. My friend planned to pick me and my other comrade up early the next morning and take the short drive to the local airport made up of one runway and a dozen or so airplane hangars, all surrounded by corn fields. We rolled into the airport grounds quietly, feeling like covert agents. Parking the car inside the hangar, we suited up and clambered into the plane. After the flight pre-check by our commanding pilot, the engines fired up, and we rolled down the runway then soared toward our destination. Once in the air, our crazy-ass friend's brother, our pilot, informed us that he had one dream to fulfill, flying under a colossal steel arch bridge. Designed by C.A.P. Turner, this Turner truss bridge loomed majestically 185 feet above the river, a breathtaking sight.

"What?" I asked again, "What?" as I sat in the co-pilot seat next to him. Without time to discuss, we were approaching the bridge and with engines roaring, we descended, slicing through like a rock fired from a slingshot. A chemical was released in my body that moment, something powerful and intense, a euphoric feeling of elation I had never felt before. I knew right then, I needed more. The thrill was palpable as we zoomed underneath with boats scattering the river below on our way to South Dakota, a candy store of fireworks awaiting us. I couldn't believe what had just happened as our pilot just smiled and we continued on our flight without anyone saying a word.

Touching down, we exited the plane like businessmen ready to close the deal of the century. It was a sight to behold seeing stacks of fireworks packed into a long airplane hangar just off to the side of where we landed. Why fireworks were being sold at a municipal airport, I have no idea but we didn't care. With shopping carts ready to fill, I randomly decided to go to the left side of the building. My other friend headed straight, and the other guys covered the right side, grabbing everything we could, from bottle rockets to bricks of firecrackers, cherry bombs, M-80s, smoke bombs, Roman candles and more. We splurged like kids in a candy store (well, we were kids) with all the savings we had. Packed to the brim, we barely squeezed back into the Cessna airplane.

Wheels up again and as we were flying home, hearts pounding, we glimpsed flashing lights near our tiny airport below. Panic set in, what now, I thought. As we taxied over to the hangar, the engines were cut and we climbed out of this fire hazard in the sky. Authorities awaited and greeted us when we landed. What a sight: three kids just barely old enough to drive a car and our friend's older brother, the pilot. Unbelievably, they only questioned our pilot about the bridge incident. No search of the plane! Luck was on our side as we waited for them to leave then in a rush moved our stash of goods from the plane to the cars. Sadly, our fearless pilot, once a hero of the skies, lost his license that day.

That evening, as I sat at dinner, my mom innocently asked about my day. Playing it cool, I mumbled, "Just another boring summer day." Over the next few days, we quietly sold our entire inventory of fireworks and made enough money that for the rest of the summer, we could relax, go out at night and even try our hand at some romance. The rest of our time, as we sat on the banks of the river, was spent pondering what our next adventure would be.

Years later, our pilot friend reclaimed his wings, only to tragically crash with his underage lover in the field near the airport. It was a tale of high-flying dreams turned upside down, leaving us with memories of daring escapades and lessons learned the hard way.

Lesson learned:

Life's crossroads demand bold choices: left or right, over or under? Each decision shapes your destiny, steering you toward the mundane or catapulting you into a world of extraordinary adventures. Take a breath, and weigh your options carefully because the path you choose could ignite a journey beyond your wildest dreams and take you to places you could never imagine you would ever go.

The 1990's

Chapter 2
1992 Super Bowl: One Hell of a Ride

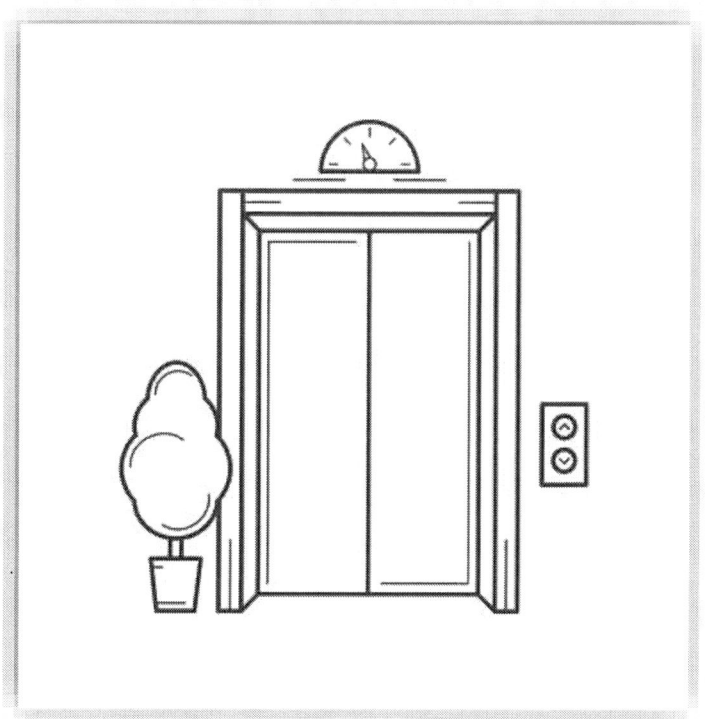

About fourteen years later now since going under that bridge, I stood with my first wife on a frigid winter weekend, the kind where the cold bites at your bones and makes you long for warmth in every possible way. But amidst the icy grip of Minnesota, something hot was happening: The Super Bowl, a spectacle unlike any other, descended upon the land. It was '92, and the clash was between the Washington Redskins and the Buffalo Bills. The entire state was alive, especially around Rice Park, flanked by the majestic St. Paul Hotel and the Ordway Theater, oozing culture and sophistication.

Picture this scene: ice sculptures glinting under the winter sun, lights twinkling in the trees as day surrendered to the allure of the moon. Music filled the air, and steaming hot drinks flowed freely to keep the chill at bay. But it wasn't just the weather heating up; the hospitality of Minnesotans thawed even the frostiest of visitors. Despite the cold, everyone felt a warmth, perhaps the kind that only icy landscapes and warm hearts can conjure.

Amidst the swirl of pregame festivities, my wife and I navigated the crowds like characters in a refined, pre-Fargo movie scene. She, draped in a full-length fur coat, and I, in my rugged winter parka and ostentatious ostrich cowboy boots, strutted into the St. Paul Hotel with a confidence that whispered, "We belong here among the stars."

Inside, the air was thick with celebrity flair. As we

sipped on drinks and tried not to stare too eagerly at the glittering crowd, fate took a turn. The elevator doors parted, revealing none other than the towering figure of Donald Trump, accompanied by the striking Marla Ann Maples. With a boldness that comes from just enough hot toddies and Midwestern charm, we joined them in the elevator, our eyes meeting theirs at a level that felt oddly equal, despite our ordinary lives.

In those fleeting moments, amidst chuckles about the absurdity of a Super Bowl in frozen Minnesota, the land of 10,000 ice-covered lakes, we found ourselves in a brief camaraderie with these icons. When they departed, leaving us momentarily adrift in the elevator, we realized with a laugh that we hadn't even pressed a button for a floor.

As the elevator descended, carrying us back to reality, we chuckled at our newfound brushes with fame. The next day, amidst a chorus of cheers and commentary at a local bar, the TV cameras captured Donald and Marla at the game, but we kept our secret close. While our friends debated their rise and fall, we savored the memory of our unexpected elevator chat with them, proof that in Minnesota, even elevators aren't safe from memorable encounters.

Lesson learned:

In New York, they say you shouldn't speak in elevators. It's actually the law. But in Minnesota, sometimes a little chat can lead to an unforgettable experience, even with past presidents and their glamorous companions. As for the legalities, who knows, maybe they'd have tried to prosecute the Donald for breaking the New York rule of elevator silence.

Chapter 3
1994 Shots at the Greater Hartford Open

A few years into the world of business now, my career was really starting to take off. This is what I wanted: more opportunity, more responsibility and more money. I would be that businessman I always envisioned I would be. Signing up for this type of life required me to travel throughout the country which meant being away from home on a regular basis. This life choice was a big decision to make as I took my first few steps down this new path. Little did I know, this was a path where there was no returning from the unknown twists and turns that would come my way. This was the scorecard I would now be keeping.

A weekend of golf, cocktails, and a medley of beer, gin and tequila shots on the side. I was in the Connecticut area with two business partners, and let's just say there were more wild tales than we can ever spill, like the infamous car crash into a historic barn in the winter with police tracking us down later that night or having to sleep in a garbage dumpster wearing a suit and tie after a day of business meetings and night of partying, stories for another time that many just wouldn't believe could ever happen.

But business beckoned on this trip, and we decided to boost our game with a VIP package to the Canon Greater Hartford Open, akin to today's plush Greenside Club experience. The atmosphere was electric as we soaked in the action at TPC River Highlands, impressing some of our very special customers that week. Cold beers in hand, we even walked the course following the many players that day witnessing these pros wield their clubs with such precision and power. It was awe-inspiring.

The morning started off cloudy but still a good day for tournament play. A few hours into it, some sprinkles came down but the pros kept going. As their shots continued to amaze the crowds, the sprinkles slowly turned into heavier drops. Finally, it let loose, and the rain poured down as we sought refuge in the clubhouse, a sanctuary reserved for members, players, and VIPs. With a pleasant buzz, I slid up to the bar next to a chap named John, that day, who was next to my stool. He turned out to be remarkably down-to-earth as we had a few drinks.

As the cocktails flowed, the bar stool next to me teetered dangerously. With lightning reflexes, I lunged and steadied both stool and its tipsy occupant, averting a potential disaster that day. It happened quickly and fast, and my bar companion thanked me graciously afterward as we toasted with glasses held high, then slamming down a number of more drinks that afternoon. Sadly, I later discovered he'd been disqualified from the tournament for a scorecard snafu.

Aside from the rain, the falling bar chair and the counting mistake, the venue was great for those that were there with the tournament's victory going to David Frost, edging out Greg Norman by a mere stroke that year.

Lesson learned:

If you want to gauge someone's true colors, play a round of golf with them. It's a litmus test to see it all: the excitement of a good shot, the patience to recover from a bad one, the frustration of missed opportunities, and sometimes, the temptation to maybe bend the rules. You see honesty in a player's every stroke, and you witness failure and triumph throughout. Golf reveals integrity, true character, and showcases both hope and achievement. Personally, I've always had a soft spot for the underdog, they're the ones who surprise you, rising against the odds to show what they're truly made of.

Chapter 4
1994 New York New York

Touching down at La Guardia for what felt like my umpteenth visit, I slid into the gritty heartbeat of New York City with the ease of a seasoned local. The Big Apple, with its five pulsating boroughs: The Bronx, Brooklyn, Manhattan, Queens, and Staten Island, was my playground. Back then, I was a wide-eyed specialty chemical salesman oblivious to the cutthroat hustle of NYC and a bit clueless to the workings of New York deal-making at the time. Our bread and butter came from the local power utility. To keep them sweet, it wasn't just about having the slickest products and services; as I later discovered, it was about "greasing the wheels" under the table with the best Yankees tickets money could buy and more. This was beyond handing out a free pen or baseball cap to show our appreciation for a new deal signed. These guys were serious when it came down to business as I sat clueless as to the real negotiations going on at the time. Each meeting started out with a discussion about the family and kids as if they were all related and looking back, these guys were connected for sure. After a full day of discussions around price negotiations and terms followed by handshakes and hugs, we were set to clinch another multi-year contract and the deal was done.

Out the tall building in New York we went, we waited on the corner and within minutes. I finally found myself whisked away with my partner in a 1990s four-door black Lincoln town car fit for a mobster to a "local" joint in Brooklyn, a place I didn't know. I soon found out it was run by a stout, impeccably dressed Italian uncle who happened to be my partner's kin. We strolled in as the dinner rush began, greeted by nods from waiters straight out of central casting, all seasoned pros pushing seventy in age, striving to offer us that "impeccable" level of service. The owner, a man of few words but abundant presence, led us to a weathered booth in the back, up against the wall, solemnly declaring it reserved for family only, but tonight was making an exception.

Sitting there, surrounded by the ambiance of old-school Italian charm, I couldn't shake the feeling of stepping into a scene from The Sopranos. With great zeal, the kitchen staff came dashing out one by one and greeted us with hugs and cheers. I later wondered how the families of Jack DiNorscio and his colleagues felt back in the day with the news of being acquitted of racketeering charges in 1986. As everyone went back to work, we enjoyed a fine aperitivo, alla nostra! While across the table, my partner resembled a modern-day Henry Hill, regaling his uncle with tales of his triumph. We were then served the finest red wines and dishes that tasted like heaven, pasta al pomodoro and manicotti that surpassed all others, followed up with both fresh cannoli, tiramisu and more toasts of success with about four rounds of grappa to finish it off, salute!

Little did I know, amidst the laughter and hearty meals, our partner was raking in millions through less savory means. As an ordinary guy, I was happy being rewarded with

19

the fine dinners on each visit to the city I came to love. Years later, long after I'd left that slippery world behind, the truth came to light: shady deals, bribes, and a fortune skimmed off the top. Rikers Island loomed large for some, a grim reminder that in New York City, even the sweetest deals can leave a bitter aftertaste, you better beware.

Lesson learned:

Always keep your back to the wall. You never know who is behind you.

Chapter 5
1995 Packing MP5's in Kuwait

I had proven myself well on the domestic stage and was now offered a new direction I could take. My missions would change and would be wider in scope on a global platform is where I was offered to go. Thinking about this new life sent electrical charges throughout my brain. It was the new fix I was missing as my drug of choice became the unknown. It is what I needed to keep me alive. The life of operating on domestic land, now a thing of the past.

Off to the Mideast, and bam! Touchdown into Kuwait. I was greeted not-so-quietly by two colossal dudes in impeccably tailored suits, their Heckler & Koch MP5 submachine guns snugly concealed, ready to escort me through the city like a VIP. These guys were serious muscle, and I couldn't help but feel a rush of excitement as they whisked me from the airport to my plush hotel and everywhere in between. Working alongside government officials, having these bodyguards around was more than just security, it was peace of mind. Who wouldn't feel safe with these giants towering beside you? And the ride? A sleek black SUV, and I could tell by the thickness of the tinted windows that they had to be near level VR6 armor protection. I didn't dare ask too many questions about its other features, but it was clear: this was a fortress on wheels, ready to roll through any chaos Kuwait could throw our way.

It had been four years since Operation Desert Storm with the coalition succeeding at driving out the Iraqi forces, so my paranoia may have been unreasonably distorted. Nevertheless, security practices continued to be on high alert as one could still see some remnants of the war with new buildings that had replaced war-torn structures. In some older less developed areas, bullet hole marks that had riveted concrete walls still remained as a deep reminder of what had happened a few years earlier. Kuwait, initially called Qurain, was known as a regional trade port. In 1938, the Kuwait Oil Company drilled the country's first commercial oil well in the Burgan oil field. Then, in 1990, over 100,000 Iraqi troops invaded Kuwait and overran the country literally in a matter of hours. Iraq's leader at the time, Saddam Hussein, had ordered the invasion with the goal of acquiring the nation's oil reserves, erasing the large debt Iraq owed Kuwait and to gain control to an outlet to the Persian Gulf. I continued to wonder, well, I actually knew the answer, if the US would have been involved with Desert Storm if not for interest in a lucrative oil supply, and the opportunity to drive order and control to the benefit of the US.

My purpose in being in this vast desert land was centered around helping to support the expansion of the country's fiber telecom system with products our company provided. For that reason, I had meetings with various leaders and groups of the Ministry of Communications.

After several meetings throughout the week that included people from the construction, engineering and purchasing divisions, my last meeting was scheduled to include the director of the optical fiber telecommunications group and other high-ranking officials within the ministry.

With my nerves frayed, I was soon comforted with an offering of Al-Qahwa, a traditional beverage in Arabian culture. A distinct beverage that was accompanied by dates and candied fruits. In traditional style, it was served from a special pot called *dallah* and the small cups with no handles we drank from called *fenjan*. The jolt of caffeine soon calmed my nerves and we talked about the goals of the ministry and vision for expanding their fiber network system. After a good discussion and a commitment to use our products, I learned that one of the men in our meetings had attended Boston University for his college education. While I had been associated with many students from other countries and cultures during my time years back in college, I gained a different perspective from seeing this man in action on his turf/in his sandbox with me being the visitor. It's interesting to think about how he may have been viewed in the U.S. with his Middle Eastern descent, attending college in Boston carrying a backpack of books, wearing Nikes and faded-out Levis while classmates not knowing about the power, vast wealth, and respect this man commanded in his country.

On my final night, I decided to boldly embrace myself alone into the Kuwaiti culture, strolling along the shores of Kuwait Bay on the Persian Gulf. I was intrigued by what I found, a makeshift carnival glowing in the twilight with about a half dozen worn out, rickety children's rides with parents cautiously watching their children go round and round with expressions of joy and laughter. My mind raced back to what this country had experienced just five years earlier as I gained an appreciation for the resiliency of the people and what they endured.

Morning came too soon, and my new pals, Mohammed and Yousef were back at the hotel, ready to see me off like a dignitary. We rolled out in our armored chariot, feeling untouchable. Through airport crowds and security gauntlets, they guided me like pros to the gates of passport control, where we said our goodbyes. After two more security checkpoints throughout the airport, my final examination was having a body pat down and my carry-ons thoroughly searched at the entrance to the airplane. Once cleared, I located my seat, sat down, buckled up, exhaled and closed another chapter in my life of experiences while reflecting on this country's journey, knowing I'd witnessed a nation rising from the ashes.

Lesson learned:

While the world can be simultaneously beautiful and chaotic, resiliency is critical in everything you do. The day you give up is the day you die.

Chapter 6
1996 The Pope Wears Brown Shoes

In 1996, I found myself on a whirlwind business trip across Europe, elbow-deep in meetings with a multinational company and its sales and marketing people, all while trying to launch our American products into the European market. Picture it: trains, planes, and automobiles, and me, alongside my suave French partner, navigating through bustling cities like Paris and Milan.

After a relentless week, I landed solo for an extended

weekend in Rome, a city that oozed history from every cobblestone. Dressed as what I thought not to be a typical tourist but in my trusty American-made Levis and Adidas kicks, I set out to blend in. No camera, just me, ready to soak in the sights like a local.

Stepping off the bus near the Colosseum, I couldn't help but imagine the roar of the crowd, centuries ago as gladiators fought to the death. The thrill of standing where history bled into the earth was electrifying. At that moment, I wondered what it would be like as a gladiator getting ready for his last battle in the ring surrounded by up to 80,000 people, the capacity of this impressive structure. I've heard it is believed that as many as 400,000 people between gladiators, convicts, slaves and others, perished over the 350 or so years when it was used for human blood sports. Shaking my head of that thought, I headed off on foot to explore this impressive city.

Despite my Lutheran upbringing, I had a primal urge to visit the Vatican City. This sacred city, nestled within Rome's historic center, is the world's smallest sovereign state, governed by the Holy See and serves as an ecclesiastical or sacerdotal-monarchical state led by the

Pope.

Avoiding tourist herds, I navigated the maze of Roman streets on my own until I stumbled upon St. Peter's Basilica. Sneaking in with workers setting up for what looked to be preparation for an event, I found myself alone in this grand sanctuary, a hush falling over me.

I took a seat near the front, on the left side, mesmerized by the cathedral's opulence. I later learned that I was sitting on the Gospel side, the Epistle side, that being the left side of the church, facing north where the light of the gospel has not yet shone. What must have been well over one hour of gazing at the ceiling, almost like in a trance, I started to hear the movement of people coming in and sitting themselves down all around me. As I awoke from my lucid state of mind, the organ then started to play as more people entered this site. Within fifteen minutes, the random arrival of people turned into a more formal parade of holy people dressed in a variety of colorful robes. Then, in a moment of divine coincidence, Pope John Paul himself appeared, a mere arm's length away, as he reached over and embraced the clergyman sitting next to me. Emotions swelled, tears flowed, a surreal experience among holy men, and there I was, a bystander caught in this sacred spectacle. For some reason, I distinctly remember looking down to the ground at the Pope and noticed he was wearing brown leather-laced walking shoes. Why this stuck in my memory, I have no idea. Had I had a camera, I'm not even sure I would have taken a picture as this would have turned this moment into some type of cheap tourist experience, so I could only take a snapshot in my mind of this special moment. I later learned this was the 50th anniversary of Pope John Paul that included over 700+ priests, 86 bishops, 5 cardinals and myself, just an ordinary guy.

After staying for the entire celebration, I slipped away quietly, dodging the crowds to find solace amidst a mass of tourists at the Trevi Fountain. Legend has it that if you throw one coin in the fountain, you will end up returning to Rome. If you throw two coins in, you will fall in love with a beautiful Italian, and if you throw in three coins, you will marry the person that you met. I was also told that if you throw in one coin with your back to the water and then turn around and see it before disappearing into the water, your return to Rome is guaranteed. One coin, or was it two, slipped from my hand, a quiet vow to someday revisit this city of dreams. While I have yet to return, much later in life, I did fall in love with a beautiful Italian, a Canadian citizen, while in Mexico, on the run from shadows of her past.

Lesson learned:

Sometimes, the most profound moments find you when you least expect them.

Chapter 7
1997 Party in Bahrain

More travel globally, I was slowly becoming a pro, going further and further, away from my home. With a son at age two and a daughter at age four, I was blind to what I would be missing and didn't have a clue. The cultures were changing and I had to learn to adapt. With my new assigned missions, I now found myself spending more time in the Middle East.

Two years prior, in November of 1995, there was a bombing in the Riyadh parking lot near the Riyadh headquarters of the Office of the Program Manager, Saudi

Arabian National Guard Modernization Program (OPM-SANG). This resulted in the death of around 70 people representing many ethnicities and countries. Drive time from Riyadh to Bahrain is about 477 km, so with being over four hours away, no imminent concerns during my time in Bahrain.

Less than 12 months earlier, during my time in the area, a bomb detonated near the Khobar Towers housing complex in Dhahran, Saudi Arabia, killing 19 airmen and injuring over 400 international military members and civilians. Drive time from the Khobar Towers in Dhahran, Saudi Arabia to Bahrain is about 65km, just under an hour.

My pulse raced during this business trip, knowing that I was in Saudi Arabia for the past week where the threat of bombs lingered, specifically in Riyadh and Dhahran, before heading over to Bahrain on Thursday night for the beginning of the weekend in the Middle East. While security was everywhere, I still held my breath every time my local partner and I got in the car as he turned on the ignition.

The Saudi working week begins on Sunday and ends on Thursday with Friday and Saturday being the official days of rest, and I was ready to kick off the Middle Eastern weekend with a bang, partying was on the agenda. An hour's drive to Bahrain from Saudi Arabia, no big deal, right? Wrong. Factor in the Thursday evening traffic on King Fahd Causeway and the mammoth customs queue, and it was an endurance test. It felt like a mass exodus in the blistering heat, over 100 degrees Fahrenheit with stifling humidity. After a drive that already tested our patience, we spent over 3 ½ grueling hours inching toward customs, itching to decompress from Saudi meetings.

Once we finally reached the border, it was red-hot scrutiny time, especially with me being an American and my partner, an Indian citizen living in Bahrain. After what felt like an eternity under their suspicious gaze, we were cleared to go, racing towards the oasis of my weekend stay, a hotel with a pool and multiple bars. As we approached the grand entrance, military-like guards descended upon us, dogs sniffing, mirrors on long poles probing our car's underbelly for any hint of danger. No bombs, no weapons, just us ready to unleash a weekend of pure indulgence.

My partner bid me farewell for the weekend, his eyes betraying his eagerness to reunite with his family after our intense week in Saudi Arabia. As for me, I was itching for some solo time, eager to hit the bar and lounge by the pool with a parade of cocktails to keep me company.

I would be remiss if I did not share with you that alcohol was strictly forbidden in Saudi and punishable by public flogging, fines, imprisonment and accompanied by deportation, so one can understand my excitement to get to Bahrain. The irony, of course, is that at that time and to this date, alcohol is available if living within the quarters of various walled compounds typically used for expats working in the country. An example of an expat living compound is for ARAMCO contract employees. (Arabian American Oil Company) All I can say from what I've been told is the sidiki is fine for mixed cocktails, but I don't think I would be taking shots of this stuff like I would with vodka. Recently, as of 2024, the crown prince Mohammed bin Salman's vision to diversify the economy now includes the opening of a "drinks" shop in the capital Riyadh's diplomatic quarter, though only non-Muslim envoys are currently permitted to patronize the shop.

Back at my hotel in Bahrain, after getting settled and unpacking, I made my way down to the hotel bar that night. The atmosphere was electric, a melting pot of cultures and desires. There were American soldiers on leave, their sharp haircuts and muscular frames straining against tight polo shirts, exuding a raw, primal energy.

Amidst them, Saudi businessmen flaunted their wealth with a mix of Dunhill shoes, Berluti loafers, and Rolex watches, parked outside were their custom Mercedes, symbols of power and opulence. And weaving through the crowd were stunning women, a mix of Middle Eastern allure and Eastern European charm, adding a touch of seduction to the air.

Gone was the solemn "Inshallah" of Saudi Arabia; here, it was all about "let's party." I ordered a pint of rich British ale, the cool glass soothing against my hand as I took in the scene, my nerves tingling with anticipation. This wasn't just a bar; it was a playground of desires waiting to be explored.

Within 20 minutes of hitting the bar, these hardened soldiers swarmed around me, their curiosity piqued by the sight of an American civilian in their midst. Just an ordinary guy they wondered, as my presence stirred curiosity in them. As the drinks flowed, our banter turned to heated debates about why the hell US troops were stationed in this Godforsaken corner of the world.

Official reasons in the books include multiple purposes based on the permission of each country's government. For example, one reason is to support the fight against Islamic State militants and to help advise local forces. In other cases, U.S. troops have a presence to reassure allies, carry out training and be used as needed in operations in the region, such as a focus on energy security: protect against hegemon, deter threats of external power, dampen rivalries that disrupt oil supply and finally protect the Strait of Hormuz that enables up to 30% of the world's passage of seaborne oil. Scrutiny of any U.S. foreign policy in the region, in reality, should go beyond any skepticism of a regime threat or exasperation of tracking down terrorists.

The reality, I think it boils down to the OIL! Oil, oil, oil and the position for a strategic military presence in the event of a global crisis.

After that revelation, our discussion got even more interesting. Keeping in mind this was the mid-1900s and people such as Jared Kushner were not yet on the scene. (Look that one up if you are interested)

In the 1990's U.S. power players in the region included personalities such as Dick Cheney, CEO of Halliburton from 1995-2000 and then future Vice President of the U.S. between 2001-2009, who helped secure massive business contracts during the US war in Iraq. Also mentioned during our conversation was Donald Rumsfeld, who at times worked alongside future Vice President Dick Cheney. My bar friends that night shared that, in their opinion, Donald "Rummy" Rumsfeld, was the most despised person in the Middle East beyond any other person. This gets complicated and what was shared with me that night was that Donald Rumsfeld and Dick Cheney, for that matter, were considered neo-conservatives with deep ties to Israel. What does Israel have to do with any of this? In 1996, these guys allegedly advised Benjamin Netanyahu to make a clean break to include abandoning the Oslo Peace Accords and invading and destroying Iraq. A war with Iraq would take out Israel's greatest threat, Iraq, with the U.S. doing the dirty work.

The believed rationale for all of this, as earlier noted, was to gain control of the world's oil supply and to create an opportunity for massive contracts for U.S. weapon makers and for oil and gas-related construction companies such as Halliburton that supposedly gained over $49 billion in federal contracts related to the Iraq war. After about 4 more pints of ale, I was ready to call it a day, and as I embraced manly hugs with these trained soldiers, I was impressed with the knowledge these guys had, though wasn't sure as to the accuracy of their positions until later in life. The rest of the weekend was spent hanging around the pool with cocktails in hand, enjoying the "scenery" as I counted down my hours before returning across the border for one more week of work in the desert.

Lesson learned:

Opinions don't just spice up political debates; they can also turn people and societies against each other, all while we secretly share some surprising similarities. And Inshallah, if fate ever brings me back to those guys again, I'm praying for another wild night of fun and conversation, Hoorah!

Chapter 8

1998 A Ride Through the Valley

On my way now to Ethiopia. After an excruciating
19-hour marathon on Delta Airlines (don't get me wrong, I

love this airlines), we finally touched down at Hong Kong International Airport, the pivotal juncture before my voyage and final leg to Addis Ababa. A 3-hour layover granted me a chance to rejuvenate for the grueling 11-hour stretch ahead on Cathay Pacific to Ethiopia. All I craved now was sinking into my seat with a cozy pillow and blanket, desperate to conquer the remaining miles.

Exhausted already, I waited in the lounge area. Without warning, just as I began to drift into weariness, fate intervened in the form of a sharply dressed gentleman. His news, my seat on the Hong Kong to Addis leg had been swapped. Whatever, just get me moving, I muttered, snatching the new boarding pass.

As I waited in the long que preparing to board, a summons yanked me from the line as my name was called to come forward to the boarding counter. What now? Patience frayed, I approached the gate, only to be ushered onto the jetway with unexpected ease. As I stepped into the plane, my weariness was vanquished by the sight of an enchanting Ethiopian goddess guiding me to my seat. What a break! I sank into the embrace of a lavish first-class haven, where a welcome gift bag with slippers and decadent amenities awaited. The purser, exuding grace and efficiency, took my drink order, swiftly followed by a sumptuous 5-course feast that would make royalty green with envy.

With my mind refreshed and as the first course started, I was drawn to strike up a conversation with a burly set man across from me as he shared that he worked for a Texan company called Sicor or something like that I had never heard of and that he had meetings with government officials to talk about some project called Calub involved in oil and gas refinery in the Ogaden basin. It was an interesting conversation though I was focused more on my wine and dinner, followed by a movie followed by some sleep.

As we were approaching Bole Addis Ababa International Airport about an hour out, my curiosity piqued as I overheard my new friend ask one of the flight attendants how to say "hello and "thank you" in Ethiopian. She politely corrected him by sharing that the local languages spoken are Amharic, Tigrigna, Somali and Ormo, with Amharic being dominant. I couldn't help but cringe at this high roller's faux pas. I wondered how someone apparently so successful could be so clueless about the local languages. Little did I know that Amharic was the lingua franca here too, a fact I kept to myself, amused by the irony.

What research I did do in preparation for my trip, however, was learn about the history of this fascinating region of the world and with the complexity of it all, I learned that up until the 19th century, Ethiopia was basically known as a loose confederation of kingdoms. The boundaries were fluid where Coptic Christianity was brought to Eritrea while the lowlands along the coast and the western border with Sudan remained Muslim. Many countries tried to invade and control the lands, such as the Egyptians, who attempted to invade the Eritrean highlands in the late 1800s and the Italians with their failed attempt to extend their influence into Ethiopia back in 1896. With the upcoming rise of fascism and the influence of Mussolini, Italy once again tried to invade Ethiopia in 1935 "to no avail". Around 1941, Emperor Haile Selassie had returned to the throne and with a combined force of British, South African, Indian and Sudanese troops, they fought alongside the Ethiopian patriots and Ethiopia was independent once more.

This left a problem of what to do with the area of Eritrea, and the pressure from Ethiopia now included controlling the people by outlawing Eritrean languages and moving industries to Addis Ababa. Conflict and war were a constant ongoing theme in the lands. Fast forward to 1962 and Eritrea was absorbed into Ethiopia. Then, things get even more confusing with various opposition groups. You got the ELF Eritrean Liberation Front, whose origins can be traced back to the Muslim League of the 1940s, the EPLF Eritrean People's Liberation Front, and the TPLF Tigray People's Liberation Front formed in 1975 to try to break Amhara rule as they began waging war against Addis Ababa. I couldn't handle any more self-taught history lessons so that is about all I cared to consume.

My reason for being in Ethiopia at that time was to promote a liquid retro-reflective technology aimed at jazzing up road signs and markers, a real game changer for nighttime driving and navigating those treacherous roads after dark. The Hilton Hotel, my refuge during my stay, was the hotspot for all the high-stakes business hustle, where deals were sealed by the movers and shakers. But then, out of nowhere, the sultry Sheraton sashayed onto the scene that year, a tantalizing rival that shook up the hospitality game. It was a reminder that competition exists everywhere and keeps things steamy and the cash flowing. But amidst this opulent battleground, I couldn't shake the discomfort of my cushy digs representing symbols of capitalism towering above the stark poverty of the locals.

What I didn't know prior to my trip, during the same time as my visit, something else was heating up: The Eritrean-Ethiopian War, aka the Badme War. It was a major armed conflict between Ethiopia and Eritrea that took place between May 1998 to June 2000, a clash that left me wondering, "What the hell was I doing here?"

Not a big deal probably, as my meetings were in the city. Right? Wrong. My local business partner had scheduled time for us to venture into the Rift Valley, a decision that turned out to be thrilling in unexpected ways. During our escapade, our luck took a sharp turn when we got a flat tire in the middle of nowhere, aside from an abandoned tank, a vivid reminder of the 1935 invasion by the Italians.

As we grappled with changing it, the tranquil isolation was shattered by the sudden appearance of bandits, guns drawn and eyes hungry for opportunity. Were they going to help us out? Hell no. Caught off guard, my partner whispered urgently for silence and that if they learned I was an American, I would be in great danger of being abducted. I complied, heart pounding, head bowed. With my head down, I reluctantly surrendered the contents of my coat pocket, every bit of cash and the prized watch on my wrist to these daring opportunists, fearing the worst if I didn't comply swiftly. I learned these guys had an association with a group called the Revolutionary Democratic Unity Front (ARDUF). ARDUF was established in the 1990s with the goal of uniting Afar tribal members in Ethiopia, Djibouti & Eritrea.

I had pretty much had it at that point as I struggled to keep my silence. With our tire changed, we were waived through and on our way. Wide awake now, I could sense something brewing, a kind of tension that made my pulse quicken again as we neared Addis. I sensed what felt like civil unrest as military trucks packed with soldiers with their combat gear rolled in, gripping their weapons like they were ready for war.

My flight was set for the next day, so after one last night in the hotel, I crashed early, eager to get to the airport. The morning brought even more tension; the city practically hummed with military presence. I jumped into the car with the driver and my partner waiting for me at the hotel and off we went. As we neared the airport, we were greeted by massive crowds on the roadway. Our driver hit the accelerator, and our car pushed through like the opening of the Red Sea as we entered the grounds of the airport. Curbside and near the front doors, I jumped out, grabbed my bags, wished my partner well and made it to the gate for my departure. Onto the plane I went, sat down in my seat (coach class but I didn't care) and held my breath, hoping our plane would take off soon. As we taxied down the runway, I looked out to see the massive crowds and could only imagine what lay ahead for these people clinging to the chain-linked fence in a land rich in history and with boundless opportunities.

As I thought about the conversations I had with the gentleman on the plane arriving in Ethiopia, I was reminded:

Lesson learned:

Better to remain silent and be thought a fool than to speak and to remove all doubt.

And while at the same time being held up at the gun point, I was reminded:

Lesson learned:

Don't ever mistake silence for acceptance or kindness and generosity for weakness.

Chapter 9

1999 Brown Eyed Girl

"Daddy, I love you." Those were the words my daughter proclaimed as she came running towards me out of our house, onto the driveway, into the car and onto my lap as I departed for yet another whirlwind "business" trip. This time, I was off to South Korea.

What my family didn't know was that 3 days earlier, I received a call from an unknown voice asking me, "Do you have a little girl with brown eyes and brown hair?" I thought, what the fuck and then the deep muffled voice continued, "Do you know where she is right now?" "You better be careful," followed by the caller's heinous laughter as he hung up. With my nerves shaken and hands trembling, I immediately called the local FBI office, leaving a detailed message on their office's message recorder. I had no idea if the message was ever received, and for the next 2 days, I struggled to decide if I should cancel my travel.

As I went back and forth as to what to do, the day before my flight, I called the FBI office once more only to be greeted again by their answering machine, so I left details of my flight schedule, contact information and hotel abroad. I also had a talk with my neighbor without sharing my reasons, asking that he keep a close eye on our house and, more importantly, our daughter. With his eyebrows raised, he asked me, "Why?" and I just told him I'd appreciate the effort. I also had a discreet call with the principal of my daughter's elementary school at the time, with whom I developed a good relationship, of my travel plans and if anything came up to call me immediately. She readily agreed without any question.

By the way, the school principal was a fine-dressed lady who made an impression on everyone as every day she stood outside at the entrance to the school wearing perfectly fitted dresses and matching high heels to greet the students upon arrival. Maybe that was one of the reasons so many fathers eagerly offered to drive their kids to school, as the drop-off lines were always filled with dads and their kids in the que, including me.

I made the arduous decision to keep my plans, and off I went with great trepidation for yet another grueling trip. With a good book in hand and a pillow under my arm, I boarded my flight en route to South Korea via Japan's Narita Airport as a stopover. Connection in Narita, is not a problem. Different story landing in South Korea. The airport at the time in South Korea was Gimpo international airport. With few amenities and my bag that got lost in transit, I was forced to spend a few extra hours once landed to figure things out. Had I made this trip 2 years ago, though I did go back multiple times later on, I would have landed at Incheon International Airport, a beautiful new international airport with private lounges, shops, restaurants and even people to help with lost luggage!

So, back to my situation at hand. Tired and with trepidation that my luggage was lost forever and that I shouldn't have taken this trip to begin with, I started walking

51

the dimly lit hallways of this airport as the evening set in. The crowds lessened, and my mind wandered as I started to think about what it must have felt like to be here in the 1950s during the Korean War. As a matter of fact, I felt like I was back in time as I walked the concrete gray floors and looked for any signs to direct me that might be hanging on the gray chip-painted walls. Nothing I could see, and to no avail, I was feeling defeated. There was not much here as I continued to look for help. As I turned the corner from one hallway to the next, I saw a line of old folding tables set up with hot/crock pots with frayed electrical cords plugged into the wall, dolsot stone pots and dumpling steamer baskets with a number of welcoming Halmeoni's serving up their dishes to the few people left at the airport. With an empty stomach and no luggage, I figured it best to order a dish and take a breath before I pushed onward for help. As I didn't know the names of the food very well, I was told by one Nai Nai in broken English what my options were. She shared with me the names as she pointed to each dish: MANDU (Korean Dumplings), GYOZA (Potstickers), Tofu, Noodles and some Kimchi on the side. As I made my choices, I looked over and saw an unassuming man who had been on my same flight. A bit odd, I thought and wondered maybe if his luggage was lost as well.

As I sat down on an old, rickety chair with a card table for my food, without invitation, he joined me on the one other chair at the table. It was an odd moment as I looked at him with chopsticks in hand as if to think that would be my protection if I were to be attacked. He said I looked familiar and asked if I had ever ordered food from Jimmy's Pizza (great pizza, by the way) near the river town where I lived, a mere 3 miles from my home and 2 blocks from my daughter's school! Now, I was getting nervous as I gripped the chopsticks like a butcher wielding a blade. This was getting weird as he continued to say that he owned the joint and he thought that he knew me. Well, I didn't know him and I know he didn't own the pizza place so what the hell was going on? He said, "Everything is ok and safe back home". I nearly fell into my Mandu as he got up, turned and walked away. That was it. After I scarfed down my food and decided to give up on my hunt for my luggage, I came upon a small office near the luggage area of the airport occupied by a frail older man who took my name and hotel information. I made it to my hotel that night, and with a knock at my door the following morning, I was reunited with my suitcase sitting on the ground. I ended up shortening my trip and went home a few days later. Upon my return to the office, I noticed one of the newer guys who worked there was gone. An odd duck he was, with a dark side that he tried to keep secret. Two weeks later, I found out who had made the call about my brown-eyed girl.

Lesson learned:

A daughter may outgrow your lap, but you hope she'll never outgrow your heart.

The 2000's

With all the huff and puff of moving into the millennium, the new year of 2000, I was hoping for a little less personal drama, though it just wasn't in the plans. As the world approached the new year, or what techno geeks phrased Y2K, everyone was on edge as to the threat of potential computer shutdowns, formatting and storage of data issues. Many software programs with four-digit years were developed that only factored in or represented the last two digits, which made the year 2000 indistinguishable from the year 1900. More specifically, going from '99 to '00 could potentially wreak havoc on core software platforms ranging from power grids, financial records, and airline reservations to government databases. It has been estimated that between $300 - $500 billion U.S. was spent globally on Y2K readiness to fix the errors and bugs, a diversion of time and money that could have been spent on other investments. Of course, if not Y2K, it could have been something else, such is life.

On this momentous eve, as I was in a little Mexican beach town with my extended family, the clock struck midnight and nada, nothing. All the worries and concerns were gone. For me, however, the 2000's were just beginning with no readiness plan in place. I had no idea what lay ahead.

Chapter 10

2000 In the Air, Justice Square & Missile Launchers on the Side

The past three years, from 1997 - 2000, tensions continued to grow in the region and here I was now on my way back to Saudi Arabia. Soon after this trip, a few months later, a bombing was carried out that targeted and killed expatriates in Riyadh and other cities, I wasn't too thrilled.

Finally, in 2003, the U.S. State Department issued travel warnings as Westerners could be targets for terrorists. "They" say, whoever "they" are (I hate that phrase), that timing is everything and, in this case, luck was on my side, I thought.

My trip this time was focused on working with my local Arab partners, selling our bag of goods and services to the Saudi Electric Company (SEC), which had just that year offered an IPO with Saudi Aramco Power Company (SAPCO) buying into the tune of 6.93%.

After touching down at Schiphol International Airport, I faced an excruciating 8-hour layover. Fueled by a daring streak and an insatiable curiosity, I decided to seize the moment and venture into Amsterdam for a whirlwind 2-hour canal cruise.

Dragging my exhausted self onto the train for a quick 15-minute ride into the heart of the city, I found myself amidst a sea of canal cruise options. With a devil-may-care attitude, I forked over the fee and hopped aboard a boat. Opting for a seat on the port side, front left for you landlubbers that would be, I leaned against the railing, my head on my hands, intending to catch some shut-eye.

As eager tourists streamed in, the boat set off to showcase Amsterdam's scenic wonders. Within a matter of minutes, the gentle rocking of the vessel cradled me into a deep slumber, akin to a blissful newborn in a cozy crib.

Suddenly, a booming voice shattered my tranquility: Kapitein Van De Boot, awakening me from my reverie just minutes before the cruise's end. My bleary-eyed reentry into consciousness was met with raucous laughter from my fellow passengers. Apparently, I had unwittingly become the entertainment, a spectacle of an ordinary bloke sprawled out like a hungover partygoer after a wild Amsterdam night. Not entirely far-fetched, given the city's reputation for revelry.

Little did I know, this impromptu nap would become a legendary tale of my Amsterdam escapade. After some good laughs by all, including myself, I headed back to the airport in time to board my next flight en route to Dubai.

Landing at Dubai International Airport was smooth as always and full of comforts once inside as this is one of the nicest airports in the region and the world for that matter. With a short layover, I quickly boarded my final flight to Riyadh, a mere 2 hours in the air. Finishing an 8-hour flight to Amsterdam followed by a 7-hour flight to Dubai, I was a bit fascinated, as I had experienced before, by the pre-takeoff preparations and checklist when flying in this region of the world. With passengers seated and pilots at the controls with their hands on the yoke, flight attendants made their last announcement before departure, requesting that all seats and table trays be locked in their upright positions. Great, we were good to go! Wait, not quite yet, as the speaker system projected in an eerily calm chant the Dua al-Safar, commonly known to Westerners as the prayer before takeoff. While I respect all religious beliefs, including lessons from the Quran, my thought was I had a higher risk of a flight emergency on my longer flights carrying me over vast bodies of water and across multiple countries.

Landing into Riyadh on a Thursday, I had Friday and Saturday to recuperate from my journey. A short drive from the airport to the hotel, I settled in, and the following day, I had the opportunity to explore the streets and take in the historic sites. After a good night's rest, I awoke in leisurely style with breakfast and a good coffee to get me started. With jeans belted up, loafers on my feet and a short lien tunic shirt so as to not look too "American", I ventured out, and within minutes of my hotel, I saw a crowd of people gathering in an open area called Deera Square also known as Safa Square also known as Justice Square. Amongst Westerners this place was given the name of "chop chop" square, a term I had not heard of at that time.

My attempt to disguise my citizenship with my dress was in vain as the people in the crowd encouraged me to move up front to view the upcoming public event, a street performer or puppeteer, I thought, maybe to entertain us all. This was no street performer nor puppeteer, rather, there was a dark and powerful-looking man up front by, what I could only describe as a puppet master preparing to carry out punishment for a crime by a convicted criminal. I was told his name was Muhammad Saad al-Beshi, and he appeared to have almost celebrity or holy-like status, fulfilling his duties with blade-sharpened skills and precision now that he had 2 years experience under his belt at that time. His official role is to carry out executions and amputations under Saudi Arabia's sharia law.

The Saudi criminal justice system is based on a form of Sharia that reflects a specific state-sanctioned interpretation of Islam. Executions at that time for serious crimes and even now are carried out by beheading with a sword, though now I think firing squads is also an option. In addition to beheadings, punishment for various types of theft included amputations of the right hand and for highway robbery, cross amputations of the right hand and left foot are performed publicly as the punishment.

Now up front and almost center stage, I was stuck with nowhere to go and basically forced to watch what originally, I had hoped was an entertaining juggler or a comedic skit of some sort. Surreal as it was and almost like a slow-motion movie, it happened quickly and fast. My breath was taken from me as I went down on one knee. I almost passed out and I know the criminal, the recipient to the blade, went out cold, no screaming, just out, then awakening quickly with the reality, I suspect, that life just changed for this now one-handed bandit. The next 15 minutes were a blur as I walked aimlessly through the streets and back to my hotel. That was all I could handle for a weekend of unexpected public gatherings, and I was anxious to get back to business on Sunday for the start of the work week.

Sunday morning, after a day of trying to process that event and the images now forever imprinted in my mind, I met up and sat down with my local business associate for a few cups of Al-Qarshi before heading out. Not a word was mentioned about my weekend, and off we went to discuss our trade business with our customers in the Kingdom. One customer needing power utility products, well, let's just say he dealt in more than what I bargained for. As we gathered for that meeting, I noticed at the table before us a brochure with pictures of ground-to-air missiles (GTAM), also known as the surface-to-air missiles (SAM). Being an ordinary guy, though somewhat versed in military defense, I identified them as Stinger Missiles that happened to be manufactured by a company called Raytheon. What were these guys doing trading arms in Saudi Arabia? Who were they? I figured it had to be legit, though as who in this country and in their right mind would dare step outside the law and risk the type of punishment I saw earlier that week. But there I was, playing it cool, though my mind was racing with caution, hands tucked firmly in my pockets. After what felt like an eternity of negotiations, we finally wrapped things up and sealed the deal.

At the end of the week, I boarded my flight from Riyadh as I started my journey back home. I was comforted this time when the Dua al-Safar was recited with both my hands folded tightly together as I had a new appreciation for this prayer.

Lesson learned:

Never bend your head; always hold it high. Look the world straight in the eye, and after this trip, I thought it best to always keep your hands to yourself.

Chapter 11

2000 Ganbei, Baijiu, Bile & Blood

When Mao Zedong died in 1976, the country knew they had to change in a big way, but the question was how to do that and save face, maintain reputation and preserve dignity on a global level. Over the years, China adopted a transition strategy of sorts from communism to capitalism, coined the "dual-track strategy," as they tried to localize market reform in certain geographic regions and economic sectors while maintaining government control and planning for many other parts of the economy.

Leaders of this socialistic structure tried to privatize strategic institutions as much as they could, with top government officials benefiting on the way, though not to the extent I think as did Russia with their select group of oligarchs as China has what could be argued to have the fastest growing middle class in the world today.

While I'm far from being an economist, instead just an ordinary guy, in fact almost failing macroeconomics in school, I can tell you I saw the changes firsthand and over multiple trips to China. I saw the streets of Beijing and Shanghai transform from authentic rickshaws and oxcarts to Mercedes, BMW and taxis, picking up businessmen and women with dreams of making it big. Rickshaws later filled the economic demand for tourists wanting to have that romantic "back in time" experience as capitalism continued to move this country forward.

I watched this transition and even helped with the effort as my firsthand experience included working with one Mr. Lee (lots of Mr. Lees in China) and his brigade of staff who all, over the years, moved into various strategic "power" seats, no pun intended, with the State Grid Corporation of China (SGCC). Founded in 2002, the SGCC is the largest utility company in the world. This company is massive, I mean big to the tune of around 800,000 employees with revenues of around $500 US billion annually. After looking back, it all came together as this group of people, my Chinese affiliates that had some level of political power during this time of "dual-track strategy" evolution, were tasked with finding, creating opportunities and aligning themselves with Western companies in the U.S. and Europe that were involved in infrastructure development. The goal of these guys was to become the exclusive partners or representatives of these money-producing foreign companies within the Chinese market. These go-getter bureaucrats and their posse brilliantly moved from government offices to the board rooms.

For me, of German blood and born under the fierce sign of the Tiger, the third sign of the Chinese Zodiac, I expected bravery and strength to be my allies on this journey to Beijing. Little did I know, I would be humbled in a most unexpected way. It happened one night after dinner as I was brought to my knees by government officials and my business associates, putting me in the traditional kowtow position, though not in a formal setting before an emperor, rather, doing so later that night and the next day while hunched over the porcelain throne, a.k.a., the toilet, worshiping a different kind of authority.

I've ventured to this enigmatic land multiple times, yet despite my familiarity, language remained an insurmountable barrier. Among my associates, only one spoke English, serving as our lifeline through gestures, translations and shared laughter. Despite the challenges, we forged a bond akin to a rowdy frat house brotherhood built on camaraderie, trust, and a whole lot of unforgettable nights.

Here we were on my last night before my long journey home, after a week of intense and successful meetings. A lavish banquet awaited, promising an evening to remember. The arrangements were set, and at 5 pm, I was picked up in an unexpected vehicle, a government cargo truck driven by Aaron, a cheerful character among my Chinese partners. I felt a connection with him as he offered a break from the seriousness of the vast meetings we had throughout the week and was also usually the instigator of making toasts and jokes at every get-together we had. Along for the ride was his sidekick, adding to the mischievous atmosphere. As we cruised along Chang'an Avenue and towards the restaurant, nestled near Beijing's bureaucratic heart, we passed the iconic Tiananmen Square. Suddenly, Aaron, the mirthful driver, veered to the roadside for no apparent reason, pulled over and, with a playful grin, motioned me into the driver's seat of this formidable military vehicle. Amid laughter and adrenaline, my companions urged me to accelerate as they pointed to an opening onto Tiananmen Square, a daring move reserved for the bold, especially non-locals like me. Foreigners aren't even allowed to drive in China, let alone on such a hallowed ground. I couldn't believe it, there I was, an ordinary guy, piloting a van, cutting across Tiananmen Square, where history had been made in 1989. It was insane but undeniably thrilling. Thankfully, I managed to avoid any mishaps, much to the amusement of my two Chinese co-conspirators, who reveled in the audacity of the moment. This impromptu escapade became yet another highlight of my journey, a wild, unforgettable finale to a week of serious business and clandestine revelry.

We finally rolled into the restaurant, greeted by the tantalizing aroma of sizzling dishes and the promise of a wild night ahead. The table was laden with a spread fit for an emperor, a smorgasbord of authentic delights of all kinds and bottomless libations to wash it all down. As the evening unfolded, so did the crescendo of toasts, each one a celebration of victory, accompanied by fiery shots of baijiu, a potent spirit similar to that of South Korea's soju or other East Asian liquors. I'd been force-feeding myself this fiery concoction all week at these banquets, and each sip felt like swallowing liquid fire. The smell alone could singe nose hairs and the taste? Let's just say if you haven't experienced it, count yourself lucky. It's an acquired taste, one not to my liking.

I was feeling pretty bold after our successes from the week, my driving to the restaurant and as I was going home the next day, I decided to up the ante and see if I could outdrink these guys tonight. Ganbei, down the hatch, I yelled as what had to be the 5th or 6th shot while we all stood together for this ceremonial-like ritual. I was getting "shit-faced" as I had also been drinking beer throughout the entire dinner with a glass of baijiu on the side. My Chinese partners called my bluff, and that's when things got interesting. After a discussion Mr. Lee had with one of our waiters, one of the chefs from the kitchen came back with a live turtle of good size. I'm talking about one with a shell at least the size of a dinner plate. Within a moment, it had been dissected with great precision and the blood was squeezed out into one glass and some type of bile poured into another.

The room went silent as Aaron and I were called to the front. The challenge, pick one glass to drink. I thought there was no way I was going to consume either of those, I was ready to concede. But then, I thought I was not going to be outdone and defeated tonight, U.S.A. pride versus Chinese saving face. I grabbed the glass with blood, held it high, yelled the word "ganbei," and slammed it down, followed by another shot of baijiu. The room erupted into cheers. I was a tiger that night. Before Aaron could grab the glass of bile to match me, I grabbed it from his hand and poured it down my throat, this time almost vomiting. With pride backing me up, I quickly took a final shot of baijiu to wash it down when, all of a sudden, it all came back up and right in front of everyone. The room burst into laughter and with pats on the back and a washcloth to wipe myself clean, I was done, teetering on the brink of unconsciousness. As disgusting as it was, this act, though not planned, saved

Aaron from losing face and what could have led to rejection and condemnation from his professional and social networks. He had won, and I had lost.

I barely remember the ride back to the hotel as I wobbled back to the room and kneeled before the porcelain throne the entire night. The next morning, I woke up feeling like death warmed over, not the usual aftermath of a wild night out, but something far more brutal. I pushed my flight to the following day, hoping a day of rest would do the trick. Boy, was I wrong. The puking gave way to excruciating stomach cramps, a raging fever, bone deep exhaustion, tremors and a tsunami of diarrhea that felt like my guts were being turned inside out. After a whole day of this torture, there was no improvement in sight. Summoning every ounce of grit, I dragged myself to the airport, using the bathroom near my gate as my waiting area as I waited in pain to board my flight back home. Luck was on my side as I snagged a seat right next to the lavatory onboard. I spent more time in the bathroom than I did in the passenger seat. Once home, I rushed straight to the emergency room, where they diagnosed me with E. coli. I was expecting something like Salmonella based on the variety of exotic foods I had eaten along with the blood and bile I had consumed, but this was a whole new level of agony. Two days of IV fluids and a cocktail of hardcore meds later, I finally started to feel human, swearing to never mention the name "Baijiu" ever again.

Lesson learned:

Reminded of an old Chinese proverb, "My head can break, my blood can bleed, but my face cannot be lost", I say, "Let the world see your inner strength and don't be afraid of being vulnerable along the way. Believe in yourself, trust in your abilities, confidence will be born, and your challenges will become opportunities."

Chapter 12

2001 A Punta de Cuchillo en

Buenos Aires

Back home for the end-of-fall and winter holidays in
the chilly Great Upper Midwest, then I was off, jetting to
Argentina at the start of the year. I planned this out perfectly
given it was smack dab in the middle of Winter in
Minnesota. I could enjoy summer weather in Buenos Aires

with mild weather up in the mountains. My trip, in this case, was two-fold. The first leg was an expedition into the rugged.

The Andes near the Aconcagua, known ominously as the "mountain of death." My mission was to help survey the land to determine how fiber optics could be installed and maintained. Then came the flip side of my adventure, trading hiking boots for a sharp suit and diving into the cutthroat business hub of Buenos Aires. Amidst the skyscrapers and bustling streets, danger lurked closer than I expected. The concrete jungle of Buenos Aires was just as treacherous as the icy slopes of Aconcagua, with its own brand of high-stakes risks and rewards.

Sitting in my office one day, I took a call from someone at a company involved in connecting the world through the use of fiber optics. Now defunct, Global Crossing was founded by a guy by the name of Gary Winnick, one of the richest dudes in Los Angeles at the time. These were the times of the "decade from hell" when corporate greed in many cases was driven by imperial style CEOs with banks supporting them that seemed to have a free pass when it came to corporate governance.

Companies like Enron Corporation, for example, though not related, went down hard just around 11 months after my trip, followed by Global Crossing, my host company while in Argentia, filing bankruptcy a few months later, in January of 2002. These guys were global players, and this bankruptcy was the fourth largest in U.S. history when, at an earlier time, this early fiber optic network company, founded in 1997 and finally defunct in 2011, was valued at $20 U.S. billion. Though Winnick was one of the most vilified executives at that time in corporate America, the Securities and Exchange Commission elected not to file charges against him after a three-year long investigation. In fairness to Winnick, it was thought by many that the evidence demonstrated that he acted lawfully and properly while at the helm of Global Crossing.

When Global Crossing was founded, the demand for bandwidth to help people surf the information highway seemed endless. To help meet that demand, the company was building a fiber optic network, installing fiber cable eventually linking over 200 major cities in some 27 countries. The shortfall? Not enough customers signed on to support Winnick's vision and pay off. Sadly, the company's overall goals fell short, and they were forced to admit that they may have been too ambitious just like the project in Argentina, I was later to learn.

After a few days of conversations, arrangements were made and off I went to Buenos Aires, where I met my Global Crossing contact, an American guy, a large, heavyset man who welcomed me upon arrival. After a night in the city with dinner to get acquainted, we were off to Mendoza the following morning, a mere 2-hour flight. His name escapes me now, but I recall how we synchronized our travel plans around his insatiable appetite. Touching down in Mendoza, we indulged in a robust lunch featuring platters of empanadas and a generous helping of locro, Argentina's famed hearty stew. Fueled up and armed with a stash of snacks, we eagerly embarked on our four-hour car journey into the mountains. If you ever get the chance to take this drive, do it. The views are stunning as you wind up through Ruta Nacional 7 towards the Paso Internacional Libertadores border. While tourists in the area focused on hiking the trails and taking in the sights, our purpose was to survey the landscape along the mountain roads, stopping at strategic peaks and aside various tunnels to determine how fiber optics could be installed and protected in this type of environment. After a day of working at an altitude of around 4,000 meters, we worked our way back down the mountains, flew back to Buenos Aires and checked into our hotel in preparation for a meeting in the city the following day.

Being my first time in Buenos Aires, I didn't have a clue as to my surroundings though our hotel was located a few blocks off the street of Calle Estados Unidos, a short taxi ride to our business meeting location. After a restful night's sleep, I met my new friend for a hearty breakfast. I gobbled up some facturas and tostadas with jam and cream cheese, along with my favorite morning drink, Diet Coke. (I settled for the local version, Coca Lite)

With my computer bag in hand that included my wallet, passport and other personal items and another bag with a screen projector over my shoulder, we made our way, a 5-minute walk street side to Calle Estados Unidos to waive down a taxi. Just then, my travel partner realized he left his bag back at the hotel. As he went for his belongings, I stood alone with 2 bags, deciding to place them on the ground, one each aside of me, a classic rookie mistake.

Within seconds, I was approached by a disheveled-looking guy with long black hair, sporting a stubble that hinted to a wild streak, wearing jeans, work boots, and a black hoodie. Before I could react, he flashed a knife, pressing it against my side with a manic gleam in his eyes. My heart raced as I raised my hands in surrender, silently conveying I had nothing worth his time. The encounter was swift and intense, a dance of danger that unfolded in a matter of seconds. As he slinked away, my eyes darted down to find that my computer bag had vanished as if by magic. Panic surged through me. I scanned frantically in every direction, desperate to catch a glimpse of the thief. It was clearly a two-person job. Across the street a flower stand and a shoe shine booth stood witness. I questioned both vendors as they kept their heads down, not wanting to be involved.

Realization set in, I had been duped and was screwed as my passport was part of the heist, so my upcoming flight seemed impossible the next day. Despite the looming meeting and the impending departure of my Global Crossing contact, I struggled to maintain composure. Trapped in a foreign land, my fate was uncertain. I was left to confront a grim reality: I was stranded without a way out. I canceled my flight and contacted the American Embassy with a personal visit the following day. After being greeted by one of the front counter attendants, they addressed my concern like a common day event, like taking my order at a fast-food restaurant. After filing out some paperwork and waiting another few days, I was issued a temporary passport to get me back home, thanks to a guy by the name of David Hodge. I think he has risen among the ranks and now serves as Consul General in Brazil. Where ever he may be, he gave me my ticket out and I'm thankful to this day.

Lesson learned:

While the roads through the peaks and valleys of life may be frightening, resilience, determination, and moving forward by taking one step at a time can reveal the beauty of what lies ahead. Don't ever give up on what is important to you.

Chapter 13

2001 Smoke Over the Water

Did you know that Deep Purple, the English rock band's song Smoke on the Water has nothing to do with smoking marijuana, weed, pot, reefer, grass, cope, gangster, boom, ganja, skunk, kif, blunt, baby bhang, bammy, bo-bo, bomber, ding, gasper, jay, giggle smoke, dinkie dow or Aunt Mary as many have come to believe?

To correct any misinterpretations, it was actually inspired and created based on true events chronicling the fire at the Montreux Casino on the shoreline of Lake Geneva in Montreux, Switzerland, where it caught fire during the Frank

Zappa concert in 1971. I had spent time roaming this beautiful Swiss municipality and the surrounding area nearby in Chamonix, France, during "business" trips in the late 1990s, always reminding me of that day. Great Jazz festival every year in July in Montreux, sitting near the shoreline listening to music and then in the winter season is the opportunity to enjoy incredible wines, dining and skiing up around Chamonix - Brevent/Flegere with views of Mont Blanc. If you want an incredible dining experience, try Le 3842. I'll save that story for another time. It didn't end well.

Back to Frank Zappa and his concerts. He and his band were already known for insane concerts where some concert goers used the phrase "burning the house down" to describe their concert experience. Ironically, "Burning Down the House" was a song written by David Byrnes, lead singer of the Talking Heads, that had nothing to do with arson and fires. Rather, that song and title were more of a metaphor for destroying the safeness entrapped inside oneself or an expression of liberation and breaking free from being held back.

For those at the Zappa concert in Montreux, little did they know, that year in December, it all came true. Rumor has it, a fan had shot a flare gun that started the fire iconically named "Swiss Cheese/Fire". The flare hit the roof and sparked some wood from the old building, and the fire spread quickly. Others claim that a kid threw some lite matches into the air that got stuck into the low ceiling, starting the blaze. Regardless, the fire spread fast, and people who were trapped up front used the large glass windows as their exit as they were smashed to pieces while people started to jump to the ground from one floor up. Fortunately, though there were some serious injuries, there was no loss of life. Shortly after the fans had made their exit, the heating system in the building exploded, ensuring that the building would be left in smoldering ashes. At that exact same time, there happened to be another group in Montreux by the name of Deep Purple. Ian Gillan, the lead singer for the band, was inspired to write a song based on witnessing the casino going up in flames as smoke on the water floated across Lake Geneva. He started to write the lyrics about going out to a Swiss town and his group being at the best place around as they witnessed the casino that was burning down.

Fast forward from 1971 to 2001 and we are back in the small quaint river town in Minnesota. My first wife at the time had dived into the world of retail sales, chasing the trend of cottage/log furniture and accessories, which was scorching hot in the market at that time. While her sales were up and down like a roller-coaster, I wasn't exactly thrilled about being involved, but hey, it kept her occupied and it was amusing to be part of this retail buzz by the river. Sometimes, I'd lend a hand but my heart, when not with our children, was elsewhere, globetrotting, rubbing shoulders with movers and shakers in cities across the world. That was my scene.

Then, one fateful early morning, the phone rang. I was awakened from a call by my old friend Bob, a volunteer fireman for the city. His first words were, "Turn on the T.V. and be prepared for what you are going to hear." He then went on to say, "You better get down to your wife's store pronto. It's going up in flames, and the entire city block may go up as well." "Fuck", I thought, "What's next?" As my friend Bob was sharing the news with me, I turned the T.V on just in time to see a group of news reporters already on the scene describing the chaos unfolding downtown. The first words I heard one reporter squawked was, "At this time, it is unknown how the fire started, and, the owners have a lot

84

of explaining to do." "Are you fucking kidding me?" I yelled as I threw on my pants and a t-shirt as I raced my car into the valley. Driving the short route along the river, I saw a sinister haze drifting over the valley, not the serene mist of dawn, but instead, a grim charcoal cloud of destruction. The smoke was rolling down the river, but in this case, I wasn't headed to a Creedence Clearwater Revival (CCR) or Tina Turner & Ike concert. I was here to find out what the hell was going on and likely to do some damage control.

I slammed on the brakes, skidding to a stop at the barricade, my adrenaline pumping. Swinging the car door wide, I leaped out and tossed it into the park. Reporters and camera crews scrambled for the best angles, hungry to broadcast every sizzling detail of this red-hot scene. Ignoring the chaos, I ran past the news trucks as I was waived to come over by the fire chief and my friend Bob as the fire continued to rage. It was touch and go as the flames nipped at the neighboring shops with adjoining walls on this 100-year-old city block. The chief said there was nothing I could do right now other than wait and hope that his crew could wrestle the blaze to the ground before it spread any further. For two grueling hours, they battled, sweat mixing with smoke as they fought to save what was left, and finally, the fire was out. What was left of the front windows now provided an opening for smoke and smolder to spew out from the inside while water dripped off the rooftop. It was quite a scene. There was smoke damage to the shops on the left and right as the remaining shops on the block were thankfully spared. Looking down the street the ashy water rolled down towards the river as the smoke started to clear. The crowd applauded and cheered as the firefighters took off their gear and started to roll up the hoses, convinced that the flames were dead.

My buddies at the firehouse said to just wait until the cause of the fire could be determined, and then the insurance company would take it from there. With a tattoo shop to the left and a seamstress repair to the right, I thought possibly it was a targeted hit though I wasn't sure as I hadn't spent much time there since when it was opened a few years earlier. There were talks that someone may have taken a contract to take out the tattoo shop owner and that they torched the wrong shop, a rumor that spread through the valley like wildfire though never confirmed.

My wife's business was a passion project, but I knew I had to get to the bottom of things. After some digging into the financials, I did learn that the store was burning cash faster than wildfire spreads. It was a hobby at best and an expensive one at that. My curiosity turned into a raging inferno as the financial disaster burned a hole in my wallet and my patience. Needless to say, I wasn't happy. As I awaited the results from the investigator and while I questioned my, at that time, wife like an interrogator about the situation, I decided it was time to put my own detective hat on and do some digging. What I uncovered left me seething with fury, I was on fire. The business was hemorrhaging cash, and to add fuel to the fire, it was grossly underinsured. There would be no insurance payout to cover the inventory lost in the blaze, it had literally gone up in smoke. What remained reeked of failure was a total and utter disaster.

I had to do something, so I took matters into my own hands and headed back to the "scene of the crime." Determined to unravel the mystery, I navigated through the charred remains of the shop floor, feeling gritty ash underfoot. Finally, I reached the back to a door leading to a narrow, dimly lit alleyway, a secret passage used by shop owners to start their day. As I moved through the store, walls and ceiling stained with soot, an unexpected calm washed over me. It was like a profound shift in my life, with new adventures beckoning from beyond that door. A big chapter in my life was closing with new seasons that lie ahead.

Back to my reality of the moment and not knowing what I was looking for, I decided to climb up to the top of the roof from the shop across the alley. What I found shocked me. A red flannel shirt and a small red plastic gas can half-filled. Could it be that this was a hit? Or, was it some crazy pyromaniac looking for a thrill or worse yet, was this a way to get rid of the business, a real setup? As the shop was underinsured, I knew my wife at that time couldn't have anything to do with it as there was no incentive here, and I knew she was devastated. I did learn that she had negotiated a number of deals with various local craftsmen and that part of the inventory that was lost was on consignment from these artists. Was it possible they hit payday from this event? I wasn't sure, and I wasn't in a position to make accusations. What I did know was that this shirt and gas can must have had something to do with the blaze. I was on the right track.

At about the same time, results from the investigation revealed that the fire had apparently started from the back of the store near the alley and that a faulty electrical plug had shorted out, acting as the source of ignition and lighting the blaze. I thought how odd, given what I had found. With a gas can and a flannel shirt in hand, I marched over to the fire station to share my findings. As I laid out the evidence, my theory was smothered, I was told to just let things be as the town didn't need this type of publicity. I protested as I wanted the truth and again was told to just let it be. Finally, with great reservation, I decided to just let this all be.

It is commonly known that Paul McCartney wrote the song Let It Be with the belief that it was inspired by a song based on his mother, Mary, who had earlier died and in a dream was reassuring him that things were going to be alright. Another theory is John Lennon helped McCartney write the song, and yet another theory is the song came from Mal Evans, one of the Beatles right-hand men who came to McCartney in a vision, and Mal was just standing in front of him saying, "Let it be." Whatever the origin is behind the song, every time I hear it, I'm reminded of that day when there was the smoke over the water on that river as I came rolling into town, when I was told that a fire was burning down the building and I had to just let things be.

Lesson learned:

Unexpected loss and events can be painful, while at the same time, upheaval in life can push one towards transformation, depending on how we respond to it. It can carry powerful messages of change and renewal through a need for release and acceptance and bring about awareness in one's life. For me, I was still on my journey.

Chapter 14

2002 Back in Beijing, KTV's

With a whirlwind of changes brewing at home. I also made a bold shift from navigating the labyrinth of dealing with global telecom giants and bureaucratic government utility companies to diving into the seductive realms of secure access control, national ID programs, and government passport solutions across the globe. They say it's not just about what you know but who you know as that mantra began to play out vividly in my life, for better or for worse. Every decision became a fork in the road, shaping my path as new chapters unfolded. My world transformed into a high-stakes game of high-tech intrigue, where government bureaucrats and leaders of top businesses wielded power like modern-day titans, each hungry for a slice of the action. Not only were they playing for keeps, but they played hard, as I soon discovered firsthand.

I found myself back in the global arena, from the neon-lit streets of Shanghai to the opulent skyscrapers of Dubai, with Africa's wilds in between. The new players I rallied with included government officials and corporate bigwigs who played hardball. Yet, beneath the high polished facades, they were just like anyone else, as my experience always reminded me.

Before setting foot in my own new company's offices, I was jetting off to Beijing, ready to meet my American counterparts, cozy up to local partners, and schmooze with the government honchos who held the purse strings. Days were filled with meetings that blended seamlessly into lavish banquets. And when the official business wound down, the real fun began, karaoke bars echoing with our off-the- record escapades, flowing booze, beer and friendly singing companions to spice up the night.

As I was now in the final process of being freed from the bonds of holy matrimony, my inhibitions were slipping away like silk in a sultry breeze. Nothing was holding me back. In this exotic yet strangely familiar land that I had now been to many times, I found myself immersed in a game where everyone played for high stakes. Initially, our dinners were tame, filled with discussions about families and cultural differences between China and the U.S. But as the nights wore on, a transformation took place. Our conversations became bolder, laced with innuendo and the thrill of what was to come that eventually led us to a secret karaoke KTV room, a haven where the selection of singing companions was as diverse as the array of drinks that flowed freely. It wasn't just about the music anymore. It was about the electric atmosphere, the laughter that came with each sip, and the lingering glances that promised so much more than just a night of karaoke.

If you ever get invited to a KTV in Asia, here is what you need to be prepared for:

1. Be prepared to drink a lot of alcohol.

2. The average time spent in one karaoke session is around 4 hours.

3. No one really cares how you sing, just sing.

4. A lot more than singing happens in a KTV room, a lot more.

Our last gathering with this crew was an unforgettable affair. Stepping into the upscale KTV joint, it was evident that our local connections held serious sway. We were greeted like VIPs swarmed by a bevy of stunning Chinese beauties. It was like browsing a decadent buffet, and after careful consideration, we settled on our picks: a lineup of six exquisite companions. As for drinks, I braced myself for more baijiu, but to my delight, these guys were aiming higher. They brought out the top shelf whisky and scotch, bottles aplenty, with Tiger beer on standby for good measure. The night promised to be wild, with each sip this time igniting the flames of excitement and anticipation.

For singing, if you can belt out John Denver's "Country Roads", Bryan Adams, "Everything I Do," or Lionel Richie's "Say You Say Me," you can make yourself a star for the evening. While the laughter and joking were contagious, the singing was serious for some of these guys, even though they wouldn't admit it. Listening to a country song sung with a Chinese accent is something to behold. As each song finished, our group would applaud and cheer, hoping secretly no encores would be performed. For me, I was more interested in our female friends, though I did sing a version of Proud Mary, reminding myself that I had just left a good job and was working for a new guy 24/7, which of course, then reminded me of the store fire I had recently dealt with. My singing wasn't great but everyone cheered me on. Like high school kids at a party, we played dice games, coin games, and drinking games that eventually led to stripping games of all sorts. Everyone was loosening up. I won't even begin to share with you some of the new games I learned. I thought I knew them all, boy was I wrong.

Throughout the evening, the energy was magnetic between Hua and me. Who is Hua? Hua was one of the gals that spent the evening with us singing, drinking, and more. As the night wrapped up around 1 am, I realized the night wasn't over quite yet as Hua was by my side. Off we went back to the hotel. The morning came quickly. That's as much detail as I'll provide, but I can say while Hua is a common Chinese name, the meaning represents Chrysanthemums, beautiful flowers that are often planted in the fall, and how beautiful she was. We never went to sleep.

After a late Saturday morning start, I met my U.S. counterpart for breakfast while most people were sitting down for lunch. Our looks and odor were evidence of the debauchery from the night before as families and couples stood staring at us in que waiting to be seated. Working to fight off our hangovers, our waiter recommended a special beverage concoction that worked like a charm. As we were coming back to life, we briefed each other on the wild events of the past 15 hours, then decided on our plans for the day, knowing we were heading back to the U.S. the following morning. We agreed a few hours of sleep was warranted and that we would meet up around 5 pm for dinner, a few beers, and watch some soccer at one of the local bars/restaurants. Indeed, it would be an early night.

Freshened up and ready to go, we made our way from the Great Wall Sheraton hotel, just across the road, to an authentic local restaurant, TGI Fridays to be exact. Clearly, we were ready for a taste of home as we sat down in this familiar setting and reviewed the American-style menu. No Peking duck or wonton soup tonight. Rather, a juicy burger, fries, and a few beers, just what the doctor ordered. As fate, luck, or destiny would have it, we eyed up 2 Eastern European hotties sitting across the bar. Hot beyond belief, they were hanging out in Beijing in this Western U.S. establishment. We abandoned what was left of our burgers and fries and made our way to them on the other side of the bar. Searching for a pickup line, we decided instead to simply ask where they were from as we introduced ourselves, my U.S. comrade and I, just an ordinary guy. That was it. We were now sharing drinks, creating good diplomacy, and contemplating what lay ahead with our new friends, Anya and Nikola. Our low-key night was transforming quickly as beer turned to drinks and drinks turned to shots. We were partying like it was Chinese New Year with these swim suit models. Now, one would've thought these beauties were working the night shift and we were the targets of their profession. Surprisingly, these global ambassadors were just exercising good public relations as this Romanian - U.S. international summit continued as we moved from the restaurant back to the hotel.

Nikola squared off with my partner as they started a discussion of their own. Anya and I went silent as we took things to the next level as talking was replaced with embracing and clothes started to fly. My U.S. partner took this as a cue as he and Nikola headed off to another room, I could only suspect. With heartbeats racing, Anya and I took this European - U.S. connection from the bed to the couch to the bathroom. It was wild, unbarred and as primal as can be. After a good hour and a half of what felt like a marathon of hedonism, Anya was out, fast asleep, her naked body under the linen sheets as I went to join her. Just then, I heard a knock. I opened the door only to be greeted by Nikola as she stepped inside. She scanned the room and gasped as she saw all the clothes thrown throughout the floor, then she looked at me, somewhat laughing as I held a pillow, my only form of cover. Her expression of curiosity turned to a devilish grin and I knew right then the night wasn't over. Anya, half asleep, now rolled over to look at her friend. As their eyes connected, Nikola added her clothes to the pile on the ground. These girls were more than "just friends," and I had more than I could handle. Fast forward an hour later and we had all crashed hard together, the three of us intertwined on the king-sized bed.

I woke the next morning to the phone ringing. It was my partner frantically warning me that we needed to be out the door and in a taxi to the airport within the next 45 minutes, plenty of time, no worries. As I rubbed my eyes, taking in the view from the remains of last night, the only garments I could see were mine. The ladies were gone, not a trace in sight. I shook my head, wondering if this was a dream. As I quickly showered and grabbed my clothes, I saw a sexy white-laced thong resting under my shirt, a vivid memory of the night before. I knew then last night was not a dream. As I was throwing my clothes into my suitcase, 2 children's books that I had carried with me faced upward, staring into my eyes.

I snapped back into reality and remembered it was nearing 730pm in the evening back home. Knowing I still had time, I opened up both of the books by Dr. Seuss, picked up the phone, and called home. Talking to each of my children, I read first to my daughter, her favorite, "Green Eggs & Ham", then to my son, "Go Dog Go". They read along with the duplicate books left at home as we turned the pages in unison, a connection we made when dad was away.

Packed and now with little time to spare, I made it to the lobby. We jumped into a taxi and raced off to the airport. My partner asked what I had done the rest of the night, and all I could say was "ne-am distrat" (we had a good time). I'm kidding, I don't know Romanian, of course. My actual response was, "I'm glad we're going home, I miss my kids". China and U.S. relations were now improved with the added bonus of a night of U.S.- European diplomacy. I would like to think that I had helped to improve global relations as I had bared all on two occasions. For me, my hope was that Romania would come my way again soon.

Lesson learned:

Changes will happen in your life, it's just part of life. Learn to embrace it and learn to learn from it. Recognize change and let growth and resilience come your way. Once you learn this skill, the world will become a less scary place. For me, I was right in the middle of some big changes, trying to figure out which way to turn, my foot pressed on the pedal, full throttle, not sure of which direction to go.

Chapter 15

2003 Dinner in the Emirates

An iconic landmark and representation of wealth and power, the 7-star Burj Al Arab opened its doors to the elite in Dubai, United Arab Emirates, in 1999, just before the millennium. Designed by Tom Wright working for WS Atkins PLC, a British architectural firm, it was shared that the vision of this structure was to resemble a billowing sail of a dhow, a type of Arabian boat. However, critics claim that the design from the water was created to represent a cross, a Christian influence in a Muslim country. Take a look for yourself, and you can decide. To make things even more controversial, in 2001, Dubai introduced the 4th series of numbered license plates with the Burj Al Arab symbol. Due to the conspiracy theories of the hotel's resemblance to the Christian cross, it was removed from the plates without any explanation three years later. In addition, any vehicles bearing these older plates are not allowed to enter Saudi Arabia.

As far as entry into the Burj Al Arab, if you are able to get in for dinner, a set evening menu course will cost you around $300 US per person. Throw in a wine pairing for another $250 bucks and you are up to $550 US per head and that's before tip. A mid-morning brunch will run you around $210 US per person. It's not cheap by any standards and was well above my budget. For me, that was closer to a weeks' worth of groceries, yet here I was, an ordinary guy having dinner with my Indian partner living in Dubai alongside a government diplomat and his brother-in-law from an African country.

As my personal life was unraveling, I immersed myself in work, like a warrior going into battle. We had been working hard to get these Africans to the table and finally did so on neutral grounds and in an atmosphere that they were accustomed to. If you haven't been to Dubai before, it is an amazing place that can best be described as the most extravagant, shiniest, fastest, opulent city in the world. It is a place where big business can take place alongside sun, cultural, and even hedonistic-seeking tourists. While it can feel like a Middle Eastern country, the atmosphere is more than tolerant of pleasurable activities. Think of this place as similar to Las Vegas or Macau but on steroids and as shiny as polished sterling silver dinnerware, everywhere you look. Here, Mercedes, BMWs and Rovers are like Chey's, Fords and Toyotas, while a Lamborghini Urus is as common as a Jeep Grand Cherokee and a prized Bugatti in Dubai is as common as a ZR1 Corvette on the streets of Los Angeles. I was lost in the moment and losing sight of what was important to me.

My partner, funded by a very wealthy family out of the Mideast, was running a security company covering the Arab countries as well as Africa. The guys we were having dinner with were the decision makers for a citizen ID project for the people of their country of millions. It was no small deal, and here I was at the table at the Al Muntaha restaurant, sipping fine wine at this incredible dining establishment located within the Burj Al Arab hotel. We weren't talking turkey here. This was serious stuff as each word delivered by our dining guests was carefully chosen, like a chef selects his ingredients, as they communicated their intent. This meeting was to seal the agreement on partnering with these guys, and the diplomat's brother-in-law was part of the deal. An instant millionaire, I suspect his brother-in-law would now be acting as their country's exclusive ID project provider.

With the exception of being introduced to this African diplomat's brother-in-law, there was no other discussion about family life at this table. It was strictly business. As the dinner unfolded, I was blown away by the Michelin-starred French/Italian cuisine. Trying to act as though this was an everyday meal for me was challenging. It was incredible, it was amazing. These guys, on the other hand, accustomed to this level of dining on a regular basis, treated this like a casual night out, similar to me going to the Olive Garden for the never-ending salad and pasta special. To best describe it, imagine eating at the most authentic, exclusive French or Italian restaurant in France or Italy, though in this case, gazing at the unrivaled views of the sea and Dubai.

We progressed through our delectable meal, heading towards dessert and a soothing cup of coffee with a dash of anise. This is when we finalized our verbal agreement. I was hoping that a formal written contract would follow and that our $2,500 US dinner for four wasn't a waste like unused food going into the garbage. At this point, I had to rely on my Indian partner as the real deal was between him and these guys. I was there as the icing on the cake. Just then, the brother-in-law opened up his brief case and took out what looked to be a brown paper lunch bag, similar to what I used to carry my school lunch in as a kid. Talk about putting your money where your mouth is, I think that comment came from the Brits. Anyway, he placed the paper bag on the table. What would normally best be described as holding a sandwich, milk, apple, and dessert was instead packed tightly with fresh U.S. $100 bills to the tune of $100k. I nearly fell off my chair but held my composure as I didn't want these guys to think I was an amateur. This was deal-making at a whole new level. I calmly looked across the table, nodded my head as a gesture of approval, and stood up to shake their hands as we finished up our evening. My partner nonchalantly took the bag, and I figured it was the initial down payment. I didn't ask, and he didn't share. As our new African friends headed towards their rooms for the evening, we made our way to the lobby, out the door, and awaited the car from the valet. On our way, not a word was said about that brown paper bag as we talked about the meal and the fine wine from the night. I got dropped off back at my hotel, more humbler surroundings, though still an oasis in this city of deal-making and gold, and telephoned back home to talk with my kids before they headed off to school (keep in mind it was around a 10-hour time difference so they were just waking up), then went to sleep, knowing we had just closed one of the biggest deals of my life.

Lesson learned:

It's easy to look in front of you wanting for more than you have, yet never arriving at where you want to be. An endless game. While at the same time, what you really need you may already have. I was still looking for what I wanted as my vision was slow to clear, revealing that I already had what I needed. I still just hadn't seen it yet.

Chapter 16

2004 Birthday in Dubai

I was completely free now from my previous "marital bliss," so my only focus was on my children and work. At home, it was all about being dad, attending the school PTA, being comandante of homework at night, having home-cooked meals as much as possible, and having some family fun whenever we could. I kept a low profile. No one really knew my work. On the road, it was all about business and domination, take no prisoners was our mantra.

We had won the African deal just the year before, and the EMEA market was on fire, hotter than a summer day in the desert.

Stock analysts were starting to take notice as the business grew faster than any other region in the world for my company. I was running the region and that meant I was spending more time in the Middle East. Moving through wealthy countries built on top of sand and oil, I was really starting to know this part of the world well. I jetted around from Saudi Arabia, to Kuwait to Qatar while using the United Arab Emirates as my base. Scheduled to fly into Iraq at one point, I canceled that journey after hearing machine guns shooting of rounds of lead in the background of a call with one of my Iraq partners. I wasn't ready to stand in the line of fire. Still, I wanted that business, but not at the cost of a potential bullet to the back of my head. Regardless, we figured out how to make it work.

During my time in Dubai, I was now regularly greeted like an old friend at all the top restaurants and clubs, rubbing shoulders with locals and expats who had made this desert oasis their home. I felt completely at ease in this exotic realm. At night, I felt like a modern-day Lawrence of Arabia, uniting people from every corner of the globe. However, my mission wasn't to serve as a liaison between the Arabs and the British in their fight against the Turks. No, my aim was to strike lucrative deals while indulging in the exclusive perks and pleasures that came with this high-stakes game.

I found myself back in Dubai, hungry for more than just meetings and deals. Touching down on a Thursday was perfect, a chance for 48 hours of indulgence before the grind of the work week. Conveniently, my birthday fell during this trip, a well-timed escape from the chaos back home. I needed a break from the personal stress of my reality as I was trying to sort things out. With plans to rendezvous with my partner for a celebration, Friday night promised to be thrillingly unpredictable and most likely memorable. My partner, an Indian citizen, living in Dubai, suggested a night with just the two of us. We were tight as could be. We had a history of working hard, playing hard, and when we teamed up, success was practically guaranteed. Business was booming, and the Dirhams were flowing as fast as the skyline filled the landscape.

As I waited in the hotel lobby, my anticipation simmered. Suddenly, he came rolling up in a sleek new

Jaguar XJR, fresh from the showroom, the deep racing green, hinting at its power. The scent of fresh new leather enveloped us as we prepared for a wild night out. Our bond was unbreakable like brothers in arms. He tossed me the keys with a mischievous grin, a silent dare to handle this beast for the night. We jumped in the car, buckled up, I turned the key, revved the engine, the exhaust roared, and I threw it in gear. Off we went. My heart leaped as the car lurched backward. I had put the car into reverse as I hit the gas as we surged over the curb. I felt horrible as we sat in this now, not so new car, the rear wheels awkwardly perched on the sidewalk. Assessing the damage, I had scraped the lower underneath bumper of this $80,000 U.S. piece of machinery in 2004. In 2019, the last year these beasts were made, they commanded a price of over $140,000 U.S., a significant investment for sure. After many apologies, we decided it best that he drive as we swiftly switched seats and away we sped. Off we went to the palace, not the official one, but a steamy nightclub nested in the heart of downtown Dubai. This joint was something else. As we approached the front, a suave valet welcomed us, who gladly parked our car right by the entrance, snug against the club's outer wall.

We were immediately ushered past the que of eager hopefuls and swept through the front doors, landing into a throng that could only be likened to a sea of Victoria's Secret Models fused with the essence of the Middle East and Africa. Among these beauties were also men of diverse origins who seemed to have just stepped off the runway of a high-octane Dolce & Gabbana or Cavalli style show. These stunning individuals weren't just attendees, they were the carefully chosen clientele, primed for a night of unabashed revelry, with libations flowing freely. And if the sparks flew just right, connections of a more intimate nature were definitely on the agenda for the lucky. And here we were, right in the middle of it all. I looked at my friend, shook my head, and with a smile on my face, declared, "go time". It was like I was living in 2 different worlds now. At home, a dedicated dad helping with school projects, taking my daughter to gymnastics 5 days a week, and with my son, Boy Scout stuff with the annual pinewood derby never to be missed. My life was pulled in 2 opposite directions, with the balancing act not working too well.

As we strolled through the bar, my eyes locked onto two German blokes that I knew from the murky business of global security. It was uncanny how our paths repeatedly intersected in the same cities, countries, and at precisely the same international events. This week was no exception. Spotting them sitting at a secluded booth, surrounded by at least six sultry women and overflowing champagne, they were clearly having a wild time. This place was electric, pulsating with energy. I settled in beside a stunning Iraqi beauty who called Dubai her home. Sparks flew between us instantly, and before I knew it, we were hitting it off like wildfire. My mate eventually dropped us back at the hotel, bidding us a goodnight. As I navigated the intricate dance of international diplomacy once again, I found myself grappling with inner turmoil. Outwardly, I exuded success at every turn, but inside, a part of me felt adrift, questioning my purpose and place in this whirlwind life.

A few nights later, we got invited to the lavish abode of my partner's wealthy investor in Dubai. He was the power player who had bankrolled this business venture, now churning out millions annually. Stepping into a local's home for dinner wasn't just a gesture, it was a statement of how much they valued our partnership, and the stacks of cash we were rolling in for them. As we pulled up to their gated mansion, the scene was straight out of a billionaire's fantasy. An imposing entrance beckoned with its automated gates, with the driveway illuminated by subtle, seductive lighting that guided us to the grand main house. Parked out front was not just one, but a fleet of luxury rides, a gleaming G-Wagon, a seductive Aston Martin, and a sleek Porsche, all flaunting their wealth and power. But beyond the opulence, what really struck me in a good way was the dynamic of this family. They weren't just wealthy benefactors, they were good people, each one exuding charisma and charm with a dash of humbleness that went beyond their bank accounts.

Just another family dinner, it wasn't. Tonight, the invite list included me, my Indian partner, 2 business guys from Iran, interesting, and none other than our new friend, the African diplomat we had recently struck a deal with. With the investor and his 2 sons also involved, we had a total of 8 to complete the dinner list, just half the amount to fill their massive table for 16. While traditional, only the men ate together that night as we were new guests to the home, so the woman stood from afar in another part of the house. Great food, great conversation, and an overall wonderful evening. The one conversation that stood out was around

U.S. embargos as here I was having dinner with a couple of guys from Iran. It's an interesting topic in particular while sitting in Dubai, a hub for trading products and technology worldwide. Enough said on that topic.

The dinner clearly went exceedingly well because the very next morning, my phone rang with an invitation from the "investor" to rendezvous at the marina that evening. Now, this wasn't just any marina, we're talking about a playground for the mega-rich, where every yacht seemed like it belonged in a Hollywood blockbuster. I strolled past 30-meter boats like they were dinghies, heading straight for a colossal 60-meter, 196-foot floating palace. That's when I met the investor's investor. A formidable man in his late 40s draped in a flawlessly tailored Kandura. Surprisingly, in this type of heat, this traditional dress for men is quite comfortable to keep the heat out from the scorching sun. He hailed from one of Dubai's wealthiest families, their empire stretching across construction, manufacturing, and even the glittering world of gold and diamond trading. And now, adding to their arsenal, cutting-edge government identification security technology, a field I represented in our burgeoning partnership.

I found myself one of many among the exclusive guests at this private soirée. On the upper deck, the atmosphere crackled with intrigue, and the air was thick with the scent of possibility. Faces from every corner of the globe mingled, each exuding their own tantalizing aura of mystery. As I surveyed the crowd, I couldn't help but imagine the secrets that lie deep beneath the surface of these fascinating characters as I struggled to find my place in this world.

Lesson learned:

This one is pretty simple though I continue to have to remind myself that while it is easy to get caught up in the glitz and glamour of material things, the best things in life really are free.

Chapter 17

2004 Cops in Jeans

As I was becoming more conscious of my work-life balance, I made the bold decision that it was time for a trip that would redefine "family time". I packed away my laptop and left it at home, and whisked my kids off to the enchanting realms of Disney World and Universal Studios. A week in the sun and fun with the kids is what was needed. It was early April, and we were excited to see Micky Mouse and the Magic Kingdom. This was a trip I was taking with my kids as a single dad. It was going to be a good break from school for the kids and a chance for us to just be together.

After meticulously planning every detail and sharing with and reassuring their mother, we embarked on our journey. This adventure wasn't just a getaway, it was a chance for me, a single dad juggling a global career, to create more lasting memories with my children. As my life involved moving through countries all over the world, there was some concern by some, with whispers of skepticism and wild rumors of me plotting an international escape. The truth was rather simple: I craved a week of pure, uninterrupted joy with my kids, away from the life of deadlines, homework, boardrooms, and classrooms. As we embraced the thrill of the rides and the joy of each other's company, I realized this trip was about more than Florida. It was about the magic of togetherness, a treasure more precious than any destination could offer.

Our journey from flight then drive to our hotel was flawless. As my daughter swiftly identified our bags, my son then took over and excitedly pulled the suitcases from the carousel amongst the bustling crowd of eager families waiting to do the same. Watching them take charge, I saw their growing independence and determination to handle things on their own.

117

Guiding us toward the rental car signs, the kids led the way like seasoned explorers on a treasure hunt through the airport. Through concourses and onto a tram, they navigated this airport like pros. It hit me then, what we simply needed was togetherness. They needed me and I needed them. Now arrived at the rental agency counter, while I conversed with the rental agent, my son was pulling at my shirt and pointed excitedly outside where a sleek Ford Mustang convertible sat shining in the sun. To my surprise, she handed me the keys with a nod. My son's eyes lit up as he bounced up and down with joy.

Everything was falling into place. Loading into the car, my son eagerly pressed the button to lower the convertible top, and we set off toward our accommodations for the week.

Having settled into our hotel, we relished the evening, unpacking with a sense of anticipation and a quick dip in the pool before the thrill of the amusement parks awaited us. The weight of my usual jet-setting covert lifestyle was lifted, replaced by pure joy in making memories with my children, laughter, fun, and a genuine connection. In contrast to the business dinners I normally attended, our meal that night was pizza and root beer. The three of us were perfect dinner companions, a family that I would take any day over lavish banquets and yacht parties. The simplicity of that meal revealed exactly what we all craved. It was clear what we all needed.

The kids were absolutely thrilled, and I found myself completely immersed in their joy. Good times were to be had at Disney World and Universal Studios. Day one at the Magic Kingdom was a success with the favorites being Pirates of the Caribbean and the Haunted Mansion as we ran back to the front of each ride for another go around at least 4 times each that day. My meetings with government diplomats were replaced with interaction with theme park cartoon characters.

Later that evening, back at the hotel, we enjoyed another round of swimming followed by a juicy cheeseburger and crispy fries, poolside. It was an incredible dinner that etched itself into our memories as one of the absolute best. Another night and we all went to sleep again with anticipation of the next days ahead.

We woke again with plans for a day at Universal Studios. All was going great with another day of fun and bonding; all the stress of home was left behind. That evening, we savored more delicious poolside meals, plotting our upcoming beach escapade. Days spent on the beach were filled with building towering sandcastles and playful interactions with seagulls, an idyllic vacation scene. As our time in paradise dwindled, the looming return to reality hung over us.

Full of sun, sand and great memories, we headed back to the airport, top-down with memorabilia hanging out the side. Our flight was uneventful and I rested knowing that no drama came our way, not just yet.

Off the full plane, we went and worked our way to the luggage area. That's when things changed. Waiting for the luggage to slide down into the carousel, we were shocked to see, a familiar face, someone that had believed in the international escape plot. Standing in the crowd, fifteen feet away, this was not the welcome wagon, and I couldn't grasp the intent. With my son hiding behind me and my daughter running in the opposite direction, pictures were being taken, like paparazzi hoping to score a photo for Vanity Fair. With my hand out, motioning my opposition to the camera shoot, the picture taker looked to the right, then to the left, and dropped to the ground in the middle of the crowd of onlookers. What was going on? With screams of being attacked, the crowd broke into laughter, thinking maybe this was a prank. Within seconds, my children were grabbed and whisked away. I soon learned these were 2 plain clothes airport police/security personnel. Out the door of the airport, and off they went, my children, with stuffed Disney characters in hand, into a black unmarked SUV, I watched my kids being taken away. I was immediately approached by another officer explaining that my kids were ok as I watched the picture-taking paparazzi being escorted away by uniformed airport police. What was going on. After 30 minutes of chaos, my children were brought back to me and we drove back home, me speechless and my kids apparently in shock. I thought I had diverted my global traveling drama as it now, unfortunately, had traveled with us back home. What had I done.

As the official report came in, the videos demonstrated what had happened and also supported by the female undercover officer as this was the first time in 20 years that she had to testify that nothing had occurred. Like a stage at Universal Studios, it was all an act.

Lesson learned:

Some people say quality time over quantity of time is what your children need. I believe that both are true with a balance that needs to be made. Being present and consistent is important. Tuck them in every night. Tell them you love them and when they come into your room because they can't sleep, cuddle them with love. Let them wake up to hear your voice, and don't let the busyness of life distract you from what is important. Trust me, it can slip away quickly. These types of presents can't be bought as I continued to learn along my journey.

Chapter 18

2005 Drug Runnin' in La Cruz

It had been nonstop for work for some time, but finally, there was a break between work trips again, and it was time to head to Mexico for some much-needed family time. Returning to our beachfront retreat in La Cruz, Casa de Familia, meant indulging in some well-deserved relaxation. The kids eagerly scoured the shore for seashells while we all reconnected with Grandpa and Grandma "Goo" (my parents), who spoiled us with all their love. An added bonus for me while home here was the chance to light up some good Cuban Cohibas and Romeo y Julietas, paired perfectly with sips of Clase Azul Reposado. Each puff of smoke carried away the stresses of the year, leaving only the sweet taste of indulgence lingering on my lips.

La Cruz de Huanacaxtle, or simply La Cruz to the locals, once a quiet beach town just down the bay from Puerto Vallarta, was the selected site for a luxury marina to be built to rival Marina Vallarta located near the airport. The new marina, which was opened early for "those in the know" and the local fisherman, was scheduled to be officially christened the following year. Vicente Fox was El Presidente of Mexico at the time; the marina was just a vision and created quite the controversy as the local Mexican, Canadian, and American homeowners on the selected shore line put up a fight alleging the project was getting pushed through illegally, collusion between wealthy investors and government officials, claiming the developers were stealing the water front property. Tough to get in the way of progress on that one as the marina was built, and the homeowners with serene beaches now had a marina parking lot as their beachfront siesta area.

Technically, non-Mexican citizens can't own land within 50km of the coast as described under Article 27 of the Mexican Constitution. To confuse the matter, however and as a work around, non-Mexican citizens can indirectly own beachfront land which is within 50km of the water under a Mexican bank trust, more commonly known as a fideicomiso for the duration of 50 years with the option to transfer or renew. To make things more complex, though not uncommon even in the U.S., Mexico law gives eminent domain power to the president and state governors. At the end of the day, money and power wins. In this case, the waters got rough for the beachfront land owners, and now they look out onto a parking lot of bustling cars and trucks. After a well-fought battle, the marina construction was finalized and open for sailboats, catamarans, and personal yachts of all sizes. In addition to private boat owners, local fishermen that had used this beach for years were allowed to remain in business mooring their Panga boats and using them for fishing, which was the source of fresh seafood for the fish market on the adjoining pier. A few years later, a Gringo style Sunday market was added to the mix with an array of arts and crafts from local vendors, unique food and drinks of all sorts, and a variety of music for entertainment. Little did I know at that time, there were some other "not so legal" business activities going on amidst the bay.

The family had all arrived in La Cruz on Thursday, and the next day was a wild run through town, snagging fresh produce and meats from the local vendors while bumping into old friends with plans to hit the fish market at the marina the following day. That morning shit got real. As the sun started to rise, we were jolted awake by the thunderous chopper blades of a military bird cruising Banderas Bay's coastline, low and fast. Up and down the beach, they went as they were hunting for something or someone. As if that wasn't enough, a hardcore military vessel, a Patrulla Costera Clase Azteca PC-211, was tearing through the waves, armed to the teeth, hugging the shore like they meant business. These guys weren't out for a joyride, they were on a mission.

Thinking nothing more of this, we decided to amble down into town for a good breakfast, followed by a stroll through the fish market to make our selection for our dinner later that day. At the time, La Cruz was just starting to attract a wave of Canadians and Americans eager to set roots in

Mexico. The authentic charm still existed in this quaint beach town as local business owners would set up their table of goods with colorful displays each morning while restaurant owners would sweep dust off the dirt roads, transforming the streets into inviting dining spaces where they served up mouth-watering local specialties from their kitchens. Around the corner, the scene was vibrant and spirited as children were engrossed in games, kicking balls, and zooming around on bicycles while town pets, dogs, and cats alike frolicked in the middle of the road, completely unfazed by any of the passing cars or trucks. This was their playground, their haven, where innocence and playfulness filled the warm Mexican air.

Arriving at our favorite breakfast spot just outside the marina, we were warmly embraced by Maria and Chewy, our good friends and proud owners of this delightful street-side cafe. Maria couldn't help but comment on how my kids had shot up over the past year, making us all laugh as we settled in. Sipping on my Café de Americano, the parents enjoying their Café de Ollas, and the kids happily slurping on batido de fresas, we perused the menu chalked up on the street side board. We couldn't help but start to let the stress melt away as we had a few weeks to decompress in this special town embedded in the local Mexican culture that we so much appreciated. After breakfast, my parents, a.k.a. grandpa and grandma "Goo," decided to hike it back to the house as my son, daughter and I were charged with picking out the seafood before heading home. With our palates satisfied, we gathered our belongings and headed our separate ways. Off we went the short walk to the fish market and marina. We were in luck as we still had our pick of fish from the sea as it had been a successful morning for the local fishmen casting their nets that day.

Walking with the kids to the marina and passing by the fisherman cleaning their boats and preparing for the next day, I was reminded of the famous Mexican Fisherman story originally told by a guy by the name of Heinrich Boll that was about an encounter between a local fisherman and a business man on vacation. You see, if you haven't figured it out already, my life was full of crazy and sometimes dangerous situations, all in pursuit of money, thinking that was the most important thing I could provide to support my family and give them a good life. What I learned along the way was that this pursuit came at a high price. I missed out on some things my kids really needed while overproviding on something else.

That Mexican fisherman story helped me to remember. There are many lessons to be learned as one can interpret it their own way. What is true for all, however, I believe, is you don't need to wait until that "someday." You don't need to wait until you get that promotion or make more money or get a new car or get a new house or find that one person, or when the kids get out of college or when you retire or this or that to have a better life. Sometimes, true happiness is right in front of us, simple and basic. The challenge is to keep perspective as to what is important and understand what it is to make you fulfilled. It can be different for everyone. I just know this, waiting for that "someday" is a dangerous pursuit that can come at a high cost if you don't figure it out soon.

As my thoughts continued to distract myself from the moment, my son had been jumping up and down in excitement, poking at a fish on the counter, exclaiming this is the one as it was suddenly grabbed up by another customer while my daughter was off to the side with a new friend, a puppy, wanting to take it back home. After a few moments,

I snapped back into consciousness, and after some tears by my girl and a bit of convincing, I told her that we could come back in a few days so she could play with the dog. Meanwhile, my son, after a brief disappointment in not snagging that fish, found a different one that we picked out as we prepared to head home, a 30-minute walk back through this magical town and the dirt-covered streets.

As we started on our way, a helicopter roared overhead again, signaling it was back on beach duty. Sporting my baseball cap and shades, I figured it was time for a Cohiba, enjoying one of life's simple pleasures as we strolled home. But a few blocks past the marina, on a quiet side street, things took a wild turn. Out of nowhere, two sleek Suburbans screeched around the corner, kicking up dust as they came to a sliding stop. Six burly guys, clad head to toe in black with black menacing masks, leaped out, their FX-05 assault rifles trained squarely on me. Instinct kicked in, I barked at my kids to keep moving to get them out of the line of fire when suddenly I found myself pressed face first up against a chain link fence, legs kicked apart, preparing to get blown to bits. It felt like a scene straight from a blockbuster movie. The simultaneous click of gun chambers being loaded echoed like a countdown to mayhem. Panic surged as I screamed at my 10- and 12-year-old to move faster as I saw they had stopped a few yards away as the action unfolded. My daughter then started moving back cautiously, while my son stayed near as I heard him say, "Cool Dad," as if he thought it was all a game.

I stood frozen against the fence as my cigar dropped from my mouth to the ground, smoldering near my feet. At the same time, two more rugged figures emerged, the drivers, advancing towards me with purpose. One of them callously crushed my Cohiba under his boot, twisting it until extinguished. Fury coursed through me, but I knew better than to provoke them, the consequences could be dire. Thankfully, these two guys spoke English, albeit gruffly, questioning my presence and whether I had a boat at the pier. With a few deep breaths, I retorted, "no way, not mine", piecing together the helicopter, the patrol boat, and now these guys. They were FES's, Fuerzas Especiales, part of the Mexican Special Missions Unit that had been officially established in 2001 and tasked with missions to include operating raids against the war on drug trafficking in Mexico. This elite group was capable of carrying out unconventional warfare in the air, sea, and land. Unbeknownst to me, I had unwittingly stumbled into their operation at the marina and fit the role of their suspect. After the tension of their scrutiny, guns aimed at my head, I managed to convince them I was who I was and why I was walking the back streets with my kids, just an ordinary guy. By some stroke of luck, I had grabbed my passport that day, which helped as they reviewed it in detail and made calls to verify my identity.

Finally, convinced, I was free to go as the convoy of military muscle stood down, jumped back in their SUVs, and took off fast, heading back down to the marina. I dusted myself off, picked up my squashed cigar, relit it and we were back on our way. My kids were oblivious to what had just happened as I took a deep breath, knowing I missed yet again, another bullet.

Later that day, we found out from the locals that there was apparently an American with an expensive racing boat going back and forth into the bay, helping transport large volumes of drugs set to be "exported" into the American market. Word on the street and apparently from the information these FES's had, I met the description of the

132

boat runner only later to be informed that they caught their man, a guy about my age, wearing a baseball cap, sun glasses, t-shirt, and flip flops.

My son to this day, still wonders what I did for a living, and no matter what I say, he just looks at me with a curious grin and declares, "yeah, not an ordinary guy".

Lesson learned:

When your daughter wants a puppy, and your son wants a fish, get them both without question. You never get that moment back again, ever. I'm not talking about buying everything your children want. What I'm sharing is the importance of being in the moment as best you can. It's true, life is what happens to you while you are making plans for the future.

Chapter 19

2005 Bona Nit Barcelona

I realized I couldn't keep being a single dad while being abroad. I needed to be spending more time at home. Back then, FaceTime wasn't even a thing yet, still 5 years out from being introduced. Our shared book readings over the phone were creative but getting stale, and the anticipation of toys from another country for my kids was losing its spark. We all needed more than glimpses through a screen. We needed each other. It was time for me to cut back on the international globetrotting and wake up in my own damn bed.

With plans underway, Barcelona beckoned, a final fling with global power players. My plan was for business as usual. I hadn't planned anything crazy, I just wanted to get this over with and get back home. Yet, I knew drama and adventure were still part of my DNA as I soon found myself in the midst of another international blunder.

If you are not familiar with Barcelona, let me share a few interesting facts. Way back when, Barcino (that's not a spelling mistake), also known as Barcelona, was a small city that was colonized by the Roman Emperor Augustus. Then, around 1930, Barcelona was in anarchy, with routine street battles going on between clashing political groups. During the time of the Spanish Civil War 1936-1939, that all came to an end when a guy named Francisco Franco Bahamonde came into power. He was a Spanish military general who led the Nationalist forces in overthrowing the Second Spanish Republic during the Spanish Civil War and then ruled over

Spain from 1939-1975. This period was commonly known as Francoist Spain and a time when the Catalan language was banned. Franco's goal was for Spain to have one culture and one language, Castilian. As things have progressed, today, over 70% of the population speaks Catalan, the romance language, with Castilian (modern Spanish) spoken more in the central and northern areas of Spain.

Little did I know that my American business partner and I were soon to run into some Catalan speaking locals as things were going to get out of hand on our last evening. Staying at a quaint local hotel to avoid any drama meant the amenities compared to the larger international hotels didn't exist. This included the room keys. They were old-fashioned metal, sliding into rusty locks that hinted at secrets waiting inside. On a separate scrap of paper lay the name and address of our temporary abode. Ready to meet up with our local business associates, my partner and I grabbed our keys with eager anticipation, leaving the mundane details of the hotel's whereabouts behind. Little did we know that oversight would come back to haunt us, much later, in the wee hours of the morning.

As we awaited our ride at the hotel lobby, with room

keys in hand, we were picked up and on our way for a 9 pm dinner reservation. Typical dinners in Barcelona occur between 8:30 and 11 pm, meaning it would be past midnight before we could explore the back streets as we had planned.

Here we were, having dinner, cena, with a group of local businessmen after a killer week of meetings and negotiations. These were the Barcelona connections, I still keep close, especially this one suave guy pictured here. But tonight, my U.S. partner and I had more than dinner on our minds. Two gringos, just ordinary guys, stirring up trouble past midnight in this vibrant city.

Dinner was more than great, it was fantastic. A casual evening event. Surrounded by old pals, the conversation flowed as freely as the Sangria. In Spain, choosing my entrée was a no-brainer, fideua, a Catalonian twist on the famed classic paella but with slender fideos pasta instead of rice. Either way, this dish was mouthwatering.

After what would be considered a usual duration for dinner, we wrapped up around 11:30, 2 hours since we sat down. We bid our friends farewell with promises of a taxi ride back to the hotel. Little did they suspect our ride included a detour, a night that shifted gears into something we hadn't planned, something that stretched into the early hours of the morning.

Off we went, on our way to Las Ramblas, or as the Catalans would call it, Les Rambles. We wanted to let loose. Las Ramblas Boulevard is more than just a street. It is lively and iconic, the pulsating heart of Barcelona that captivates tourists and locals alike. For us, it was where adventure lurked in every shadowed corner. Sure, it was past midnight, and the street was winding down, but that didn't faze us. We weren't going to be disappointed. We were on a mission to seek out excitement. Eventually, we stumbled upon a hotel with a seedy casino and dimly-lite, smoke-filled bar. It seemed like our best shot at keeping the night alive, so we grabbed seats at the bar and ordered up some drinks. We were determined to make the most of the night, no matter the cost.

With a stroke of fate (or perhaps just another lucky or unlucky moment), two sultry dark-haired Catalan-speaking vixens sauntered up to us. Within minutes, we were deep in conversation, clinking glasses and sharing laughs like old friends having a good time. It was nearing 2 am now.

That's when they made a proposition that left us intrigued, come with us to their apartment above a nearby warehouse just a few blocks away, they offered. With our interest now stirred, we ventured into the darker, more mysterious alleys of the city, guided by these bewitching locals. Finally, we arrived at what looked like an industrial elevator, a stark contrast to the liveliness of Las Ramblas.

Curiosity piqued, we shrugged, and up we went. A few floors up, we stepped into a corridor resembling a cross between a dorm and a den of iniquity with snug apartment-like rooms lining the hallway. What set it apart? There was an old lady sitting at a small desk with a dimly lit lamp to aid her in whatever she was doing. Little did we realize we were walking right into temptation's lair. My partner was still hungry and had taken the bait. He wanted to finish off the night with a bang.

Brimming with anticipation, he wasted no time. With a mischievous grin, he handed over his credit card to this cunning old lady behind the desk. These chicas were rameras, gamberras, at this point I'd even say putas. I was tired and ready to go back to the hotel. One problem, this meek fray lady now turned into a pit bull. She wasn't giving my buddy his credit card back. I was done. "Let's go", I yelled in frustration, "deal with the credit card later." After another 15 minutes of unsuccessful negotiating, we left, leaving the credit card behind.

With a pocket full of Euros and my credit cards to back us up, we stumbled towards a stairwell that left us back outside. It was around 4:30 am now, and we needed to get back to the hotel. Though we were inebriated and tired, we were able to flag down a taxi. One problem: we didn't know the name or address of the hotel. This was not good. All we had was our room keys as evidence of a place to stay. We told the driver to hit the gas as we pointed him to move forward with no direction in mind. Just get us back to the hotel. That's all we wanted. Getting onto the Nus de la Trinitat, the major highway interchange constructed in 1992 for the 1992 Summer Olympics we figured would give us a view of where we needed to go. For another 15 minutes, our driver endured us, drunken fools, in the back of his taxi. He was losing patience fast. Atop of this road of interwoven bridges, we could see the area of our hotel, but our time was up. With no warning, in the middle of the roadway, the car screeched to a halt. "Sortir, surt ara" our driver yelled. He jumped from his seat, onto the roadway and swung open the back door, telling us to get out as he waived his hands furiously.

Here we stood, atop this towering roadway, taking in the views of Barcelona as the sun was beginning to rise. It was an odd moment of serenity. The city was starting to wake as the cool morning air brought us to our senses. We now had our hotel in sight. We just had to figure out how to get there. With traffic still light, we were able to stumble our way through the maze of concrete, finally making it to our hotel. Beat and exhausted, we stepped into our rooms. It was nearing 6 am as I fell onto the bed. I shook my head as I couldn't believe why this kept happening to me. Drama after drama. The excitement was getting old, a night I didn't want to remember. I was creating situations of unpredictability to feel alive. My work was a bore and I was looking for something more. A thrill seeker looking for excitement, I was throwing myself into a novelty of situations that offered me jolts of stimulus to the brain. My safe zone was constantly turning into a hot zone as my innate search for fulfillment was constantly leading me in the wrong direction. Being able to navigate the world's cities, I still couldn't find my way.

Lesson learned:

The search for fulfillment can be confusing. While many want to provide you with the answer to "life", the fact is that you need to figure out what's important to you. Find your purpose, find your meaning, and don't ever let it go.

Chapter 20

2006 Blackjack with the Boys

As I ditched my jet-setting, high-flying lifestyle for something a bit more grounded, I figured sticking to domestic travel would be a breeze and allow me to be closer to home, something that was desperately needed. I could make this work: one night, I'm savoring a sizzling dinner in Los Angeles, and by the crack of dawn, I'm back, cheering on my daughter at her gymnastics competitions. Jetting from New York to Miami to Seattle? Child's play. I could handle that with my eyes closed. This new setup was going to work well, just with a little less intensity and a lot more balance for the family. The odds were going in my direction.

No way could drama or crazy adventure come my way now that I was back on American ground. However, my DNA for adventure was still stirring. Like an addiction, I needed my fix. I'm not joking. Sensation seeking is a real thing linked to the neurotransmitter dopamine, a chemical that carries messages in the brain that make us feel good. Within the DNA, scientists have narrowed it down to around a dozen mutations within genes that are related to dopamine. It's also believed that a single-nucleotide polymorphism or SNP can also help identify sensation seekers. It's a bit confusing as a mutation is defined as any changes in a DNA sequence away from normal while a single-nucleotide polymorphism, or SNP as the experts refer, is a variation at a single position in a DNA sequence among individuals. Either way, it's real, and I think I have it.

I was rolling with two of my closest partners in crime. Our bond is tighter than a vice, a trifecta of chaos and camaraderie. This was no ordinary crew; this was a trifecta of mayhem: the "initiator," a work partner from the past; the

144

"cleaner," a long-time trusted partner as well, this guy was 6'4" muscle who could deal with any trouble that dared cross our path; and myself, the "negotiator," weaving deals from every corner of the globe. We had a formula for mayhem that was as explosive in business as it was in pleasure.

Our trip the month before took us to the streets of L.A., crashing a club that was clearly not in our favor. We ended up at odds with the wrong crowd as we abruptly got booted out by bangers and their burners but we survived thanks to our "cleaner," who, true to his name, cleared the path for our escape.

Now, here we were in Vegas, where the trip was as easy as it was predictable. The odds were in our favor. A few posh dinners, a couple of meetings, and plenty of time to test our luck at the tables. We'd just wrapped up a dinner with a gaggle of greenhorns from Portland eager to break into the security game and still had plenty of fuel left in the tank, so we headed straight to the Hard Rock Hotel and Casino, looking to push our limits. Though I'm not one for the gambling scene, preferring the odds at the business table where I was the one holding all the cards, tonight I was willing to roll the dice. At the bar, we started, Red Bull and vodkas to fuel our spirits, and we were ready to go. Drinks were disappearing, shots were flying, one, two, three, and our adrenaline was through the roof. Here we go again, I thought. Our trio of trouble magnets drew a crowd wherever we roamed. We had our own entourage and now everyone wanted a taste of our recklessness. The atmosphere around us was electric, a swirling vortex of chaos that pulled everyone into our orbit.

After a wild mix of bar tricks, chants, and cheers, our newly formed crew stormed through the casino as we headed towards the high roller section, VIP to be exact. An ordinary guy, I wasn't too keen on splurging big bucks, but the adrenaline hit me hard. My dopamine levels started to surge. I couldn't control it, and my bros and I were hooked. It was like living in a never-ending loop of thrills and drama. Groundhog Day over and over wherever we went. From casinos to yachts to private rooftop parties overlooking Miami's South Beach, now, it was happening again. This time, Vegas was our playground. I found myself on a stage of sorts, being cheered on by a group of onlookers as I swaggered toward a blackjack table. As I moved through a crowd of players, my confidence oozing from every pore, I slid in between some unique characters that welcomed me like an old friend. My friends, the "initiator" and "cleaner," stood by, while our entourage of now a dozen or so tried to catch every moment of the action. I tossed a grand onto the table, feeling the rush as the dealer slid me my stack of chips.

As the crowd grew and the energy filled the air, I looked at the player on my left. "Nice baseball cap", I commented, with our glasses held high as we gave each other a manly nod of approval. To my right, a shorter, scruffy guy around 5' 6" I'd guess, focused on his cards as we all played some hands. The "cleaner" leaned in at one point close and asked, "Do you know who that is standing next to you?" I didn't really care but as the crowd grew, I figured I wasn't the one they were looking at. He leaned in again and whispered, "ice" as I looked down at my drink full of ice. Then it struck me, the guy next to me was Robert Matthew Van Winkle, aka…Vanilla Ice. That's cool, I thought as I was trying to play the cards. Then, my curiosity got the best of me as I looked to the right again. Hey, I recognized this scruffy guy by my side. He was in a few movies, I recalled. A movie star? I couldn't place him. It was a guy by the name of Ron Jeremy. Let's just say I recognized his face from a film I had once seen years earlier at a bachelor party. The movie had something to do with a gal by the name of Debbie that went back to Dallas. That's about all I could remember. Hmm, this was getting interesting. To the right of Ron was a guy much smaller in structure, I'm guessing around 3' tall, standing on a chair as we continued to play our cards. Austin Powers, I said to myself. This was the guy from the Austin Powers movies, Verne Troyer. It was Mini-Me.

It was the four of us now: Robert, Ron, Verne, and me. Along their side, they had an entourage as well. Four Filipino young ladies dressed in scanty dresses cheering them on. What a sight, me and my buddies, our new friends from the bar, and this group of characters as the room continued to fill. It didn't last long, as my chips were disappearing with every hand. I'd win a few hands, then lose even more. After a few more head nods with Robert, a high five with Ron, and a pat on the back for Verne, this game was done. I could tell that their Filipino friends were ready to play, but not at the table. They had other thoughts on their minds, something I planned to stay out of at all costs. I thought it best to be on our way before we went all in on this bet. Adamant to call it a night, I was intent on shifting gears.

I needed to focus on trying to have a quieter type of life. My buddies, however, weren't quite done as they wanted to up the stakes, asking for me to stay. Something clicked in my head as I walked away, back to my room. I had enough. I was hoping I was moving in the right direction, but the storm kept swirling around me. I had to clear this from my body, but the addiction continued to linger from within.

Lesson learned:

We don't walk away to teach people a lesson, we walk away because we finally learned ours. I was still walking the journey.

Chapter 21
2006 Running a Red

This domestic travel wasn't half as slow as I'd expected. While drama still continued to cross my path, it was nothing compared to the wild, untamed chaos of the international scene. Closer to home and with my brothers from another mother close by, I had a solid safety net, like seat belts and airbags, for this crazy business we rolled in. Life at home was calming down, but I was still aching for something more as the emptiness was still inside. I was juggling life to keep it all from crashing down. At least my kids had comfort knowing that their dad wasn't on the other side of the globe doing whatever it was he did for a living, not knowing if I would return. I was making moves, and I knew I was heading in the right direction.

Here we were now, deep in the sultry heart of Charlotte, North Carolina, gearing up for a whirlwind of meetings and dinners. It was scorching hot as it was approaching the end of July. A repeat as before but not at the steps of Sin City, this trip would be a breeze. We would roll in, get our business done, and roll out and be home before the weekend. After our last dinner, we hit the bars for a few after-dinner drinks. Nothing too crazy, but I could already feel the electric buzz of the Red Bull and vodkas combo taking hold. Buzzed and wide awake, I was on a new kind of high, a thrilling cocktail of drunken energy that I was still learning to master. With my thoughts under control, I was determined to ride the night out without crashing.

We heard from the locals that the Lynyrd Skynyrd Band was playing at the Verizon Wireless Amphitheatre that week. Being an ordinary guy, this band played to my senses with its rhythm and down-home lyrics. We missed out on concert tickets, but the bar played their tunes that night: "Call Me The Breeze," "Free Bird", and, of course, one of my favorites, "Simple Man." My dad and I used to listen to that song a lot as we would sing along together the simple words with powerful meaning. I remember my dad talking to me about the importance of being simple and humble. He then would go on and tell me that whatever I did in life, I should follow my heart as that is what I need to do. I knew that all he wanted for me was to be satisfied in life.

As we arrived back to our hotel that evening, I could see some commotion up front. Forget the drama, I was just itching to hit the sheets and go to bed. But as we approached, my jaw nearly dropped. A beautiful customized tour bus had parked up front. Not any typical run-of-the-mill tour bus, but a polished, sleek beast of a ride, a penthouse on wheels, emblazoned with the name Lynyrd Skynyrd on its side. I couldn't believe it. The band was crashing at our hotel. Despite the tight security, our earlier check-in had its perks as we were waved on through. We made our way to the hotel bar for one last drink. Walking through the bar, I was reminded of their song about poisoned whiskey and what would be my last drink for the night. Settling up at the bar, I noticed a group huddled back in the corner, those scruffy, road-weary rockers desperate for a little quiet after a night of Southern country rock blues. I caught glimpses of a few familiar faces, maybe Johnny Van Zant and Michael Cartellone? - from what I could tell as we downed our drinks and called it a night. But hold on, that's not the end of this story but it happened the same week, so I wanted to share. I couldn't shake the thought: these guys on the road, living a rockstar life. I wondered if they struggled with similar issues but on a different stage, under a different spotlight, yet maybe just like me.

After a good night's sleep and an early morning breakfast, we were eager to hit the road to get back home. Pulling up to Charlotte Douglas International Airport, we ditched our rental car and made our way to the terminal. Another story for another time, as I'm reminded of my friend, just another ordinary guy, who had shut a portion of this airport down a few years back. A simple mistake, nothing bad at all, but confusion by security thinking a bomb was in his luggage as everyone had to be evacuated, he brought this airport to its knees.

Back to my story, as I lounged in the terminal awaiting our flight, my gaze fell on a striking scene. Sitting in the waiting area like everyone else, I saw a man in a sleek black hat and dark shades covering his eyes, surrounded by a younger couple and what looked like their child. A nice family keeping their heads down, trying their best to keep a low profile. Watching this from the other side, there was no escaping for this family from the buzzing whispers and surreptitious glances from the crowd. What a pain I thought, nowhere to hide as this family just wanted to board the flight. It wasn't long before a few bold souls stepped out of the crowd, armed with pen and paper in hand, eager to score a souvenir of some sort. This mysterious man, with a kind smile on his face, graciously signed autographs, and soon our boarding call echoed through the terminal, giving him a break. Being a road warrior of sorts, I was constantly getting upgraded to first class wherever I traveled. Onto the plane and into my seat, 2B, I recalled. To my side, the king, true to style in that Charlie 1 Horse brand cowboy hat, it was Richard Petty. This was going to be an interesting ride up to Minneapolis, Minnesota.

Refusing to be star-struck as I suspected he'd prefer,

154

we chatted briefly as we rolled down the runway and wheels lifted into the air. As we both sipped our beverages, I could tell a conversation was brewing as we started a friendly engagement. Sharing our final destinations, my finish line was Minnesota while that was his pitstop en route to Idaho, specifically Coeur d'Alene. We talked some more about kids and family like we were classmates at a reunion. I'll keep that part personal and prefer not to share. However, I did learn of a very special event, a charity ride called the Kyle Petty Charity Ride Across America. This was an annual charity ride that is done to help raise donations for a very special cause, the Victory Junction Gang Camp, which had opened in 2004 for chronically ill children as a way to honor his late grandson. A camp for seriously ill kids that come from all over the country. No cost to the campers. They don't get charged for anything as they get the opportunity to be kids and forget about their problems for a while. A true legacy for children. Since the charity ride debut in 1995, this event has raised around $22 million US not only for Victory Junction but for other children's charities as well.

This year's course included starting in Coeur d'Alene, Idaho, and gliding through Glacier National Park.

Like all the rides, they are coordinated so that all participants stay together with clothing and personal items hauled in trucks with riders focusing on the open road. So well-coordinated that in many of the towns along the way, troopers, I was told, awaited to let this diverse group of charity riders continue on, passing right through every stop light as crowds of people from the towns cheer them on.

It was a delightful conversation that passed the time quicker than a 9-second quarter mile. Soon we were landing, and as our conversation was coming to an end, the king closed his story that at one time when back home, he jumped in his car and as he innocently rolled through town, he declared, "damn, if I didn't get a ticket for running a red."

Lesson learned:

Helping anyone in need comes from a place of benevolence and love. It starts with compassion, empathy, and gratitude while cultivating personal values. I wanted to leave a positive footprint as I continued walking my path.

Chapter 22

2007-2012 Status Quo

After a period of some intense soul-searching, I made a life-altering decision: I left behind the high-flying world of security for a nonprofit organization dedicated to helping others using light manufacturing and services across various trades. The days of swanky dinners, high-stakes negotiations, and jet-setting across the globe were over. My new reality was a steady 9-to-5 grind. Mornings began with getting the kids off to school, followed by a day at work, shuttling them to extracurriculars, preparing family dinners, overseeing homework, and squeezing in laundry and family time on weekends. The dramatic whirlwind of my former life was replaced with a "comforting" routine, as I hoped that my drama would be gone. It was a change for us all.

But just as I was beginning to find my footing in this new chapter, disaster struck. Later that year, I learned that one of the organization's biggest accounts, crucial to our mission, was disappearing. The timing couldn't have been worse. The company faced significant cutbacks, and I was suddenly confronted with the harsh reality of needing to navigate this crisis myself. No one was coming to rescue me from this mess. The drama had come home, and it was up to me to clean it up.

Headcount had to be slashed. I just left a lucrative business to help others and now I found needing help myself. I put myself here unknowingly and had to figure out how to get myself out. No one was going to help me. This drama was now in my backyard, and I had to clean it up.

I was now jobless, and so were a bunch of other driven, passionate individuals who had dedicated themselves to helping others. With bankruptcy looming over me, I felt like everything I'd worked for was slipping away. On top of that, my attempts at finding love had left me with a series of heartbreaks, deepening the void I was struggling to fill. It all became too much, I was at my breaking point, overwhelmed and on the edge of losing it all. I was starting all over again.

First things first as I rallied this group of recently displaced charity workers and declared, "This is our new mission!" With a shoestring budget and fierce determination, I launched a new venture, setting our sights on outshining the old company that had left us on the streets. We would go after any of the accounts this old company had and do it better. I gambled with everything, and it paid off. We won some big deals, and soon, I was able to bring on a number of people that were laid off. It was fulfilling and a charity of a new kind where I took a back seat and kept my salary minimal as I still didn't draw much pay.

Back home, my family rallied around me, and together, we crafted a new routine to stabilize our lives. Despite tough times, we adapted with resilience and ingenuity. Goodwill and the Dollar Store became our go-to havens, and we learned to stretch every dollar while embracing gratitude for our blessings.

On a later Christmas day, my son gave to me one of the biggest gifts of all. Innocent and pure, a lesson of hope that I carry today. He so desperately wanted a kid's tool workbench from Santa, the kind with the hammer and saw, while my daughter had sights on an American Girl doll. Nothing too fancy, but our dollars were still slim. The months leading up, I was able to save enough for their dreams on that special Christmas day. The doll my daughter wanted I wrapped with a bow, and thinking of a fun project for my son. I decided his tool bench we could put it together that morning. The flat box wrapped nicely, laying on the floor, looking like nothing of a bench, it was impossible to tell.

With excitement my daughter opened her gift and shrieked with joy as she held her new doll that looked like her twin. My son stared with disappointment as he didn't see that workbench near the tree. His comment stays with me every year on this day, "Daddy, Santa forgot me, but at least we have family, and that's really ok." I broke into tears as I hugged them both as my son opened his gift with surprise, and that's all I can say.

During these years, we had our ups and downs like any ordinary family would have. I sold that business, and the people on my team were able to keep their jobs as part of the deal. With this mission now accomplished, I was ready to

160

get back into the life of the security business again. The timing was right. This go around, I was hoping to stay clear of the drama from the past.

Lesson learned:

Sacrifice must come before success, and success needs to be carefully defined as a pursuit in life. I had brought some balance back into my family and was hoping it just wasn't too late.

Chapter 23

2013 Heat Versus the Bulls

I was ready to pivot and make my move as I jumped back into the security arena. This time, I was grounded in the U.S., as I kept my feet planted before taking my shot at this type of life again. I knew this game, and I knew it well. My focus was sharper, and my strategy was refined. No more entangling myself in volatile situations this time. I was in control. With no more long trips across the globe, as I did before, I could balance my work and life at home.

Here I was, a seasoned pro re-entering the fray among a new generation of hungry players eager to

162

showcase their skills. They brimmed with youthful energy, but I brought with me the wisdom of experience. I had an uncanny knack for spotting opportunities and sealing deals with the precision of a buzzer-beater in a championship game. The arena was set, and I was ready to make my mark.

I was working with some guys in Miami looking to enhance various types of secure identification and financial security for wealthy season pass holders for pro basketball games at the American Airlines Arena. That was the name of this place from 1999 until 2021. It then changed names to the FTX Arena from 2021 until 2023. You might recognize this place under another name, Miami-Dade Arena, a title it held briefly in 2023 and now called Kaseya Center. This new name is based on the IT and security software company, Kaseya, that purchased the naming rights after FTX went bankrupt.

I was gearing up for a quick overnight getaway to Miami, a pivotal journey that could make or break our play. With the kids safely nestled at their moms, I headed out without a trace, armed with just an overnight bag, I'd be home by dinner the next day. My potential partners for this project were sharp business operators with insider connections to the Miami Heat. We were hoping this deal would be a slam dunk, propelling us into the spotlight. This trip wasn't just another routine, it was a chance to turn a dream into reality.

From the airport to their office with brief introductions, the meeting went well. With a working lunch underway, I realized that the leader of this group and I were going to get along great. We were done by 4 pm, plenty of time for a night to relax. It just so happened that the Heat was playing the Bulls in town that night for one of the Eastern Conference Semifinals playoff games. Great, I'd be back to my hotel with plenty of time to settle into my room with pizza and beer and a front row seat on my bed watching the game on TV. I was excited for that night, no dinners or partying, just my time alone then back home the following day.

Within minutes of stepping into my hotel room, my phone buzzed with unexpected news. It was my new working partner, and he was calling to see if I was free tonight. My tranquil evening was suddenly at risk. He swiftly pitched an intriguing proposition, a special event that required me to be ready within the hour. I wrestled with my desire for a quiet night, brainstorming excuses to stay in. But then he dropped a bombshell, he had tickets to the basketball game that night. An electric thrill surged through me, reminiscent of a long-forgotten rush. My heart started to race as if jolted by a shot of Epinephrine. How could I possibly turn this down? I swapped my boxer shorts for jeans and dashed out the door. Moments later, my partner arrived in his sleek new black Porsche Panamera GTS. With the roar of the engine and the gleaming city lights guiding our way, we sped toward the stadium, my anticipation building with every second we drew near.

With this sleek drive to the venue, we arrived with undeniable flair. As we neared the grand stadium, we veered toward a hidden, underground entrance, shielded from the bustling crowds. A swipe of his entry card sent the door gliding open, revealing a subterranean haven. He guided his black rocket into the garage, a marvel of modern design. We accelerated down the ramp and turned right. He knew where he was going. Into a pristine parking area, we stopped. A space that could rival any exotic car showroom. It was automotive opulence at its finest with Lamborghinis, Ferraris, and Bentleys, just to name a few. As we parked, a team of staff awaited us, including a striking valet who greeted my partner with a warm hug as he handed over the keys. "This is my good friend from up North," he introduced me, and as VIP bands were slipped onto our wrists, I felt a thrill, this night was shaping up to be extraordinary.

This exclusive garage was reserved for players and elite staff, and it was clear he was well-connected. Despite his seemingly ordinary demeanor, he was recognized by everyone we passed. As we walked through the stylish hallways and ascended to the private outdoor deck, the ambiance was electric.

I tried to keep my composure as I was back in the game. I played it cool as I'd been here before and decided to enjoy the moment, knowing I would be home the following day back to my normal routine.

The game was starting soon, so we made our way into the stadium and worked our way to our seats. From the top, we descended down, each row we continued to pass. To the final level, we went by security as the court was within reach. With 2 steps to the floor, our wristbands were checked as we were escorted to our final destination. We were sitting courtside on the floor with just one row of seats to our front.

Within feet of the players, my partner said his hellos.

With the other select few that were allowed onto the floor, it was obvious these folks had been here before. To my far right, it was Curtis Jackson, better known as Fifty Cent, who was settling into his chair, blending in among this unique crowd that came to watch the game like any other fan. The view from our seats was spectacular. Just in front of us, a family of three occupied their chairs: a mother, a father, and their daughter named Julia. My friend greeted them warmly, revealing that he knew them quite well.

With the players off the courts, the lights went dim, and all of a sudden, this girl named Julia, at age 12, slowly walked onto the court. As her parents urged her on, I wondered what she was doing. She moved to the center with no one protesting, and suddenly, the spotlights came on. She was handed a microphone, and the crowd went silent. It was clear, this girl was going to sing as the start of the national anthem started to ring. Throughout the stadium, we all stood up now on our feet. This girl sang the anthem like I had never heard before. It was a moment of perfection as the crowd went crazy. Everyone in that building had just witnessed something special, it was unreal.

The game erupted into action the moment it began, a thrilling clash between the Heat and the Bulls. They went at it hard. The cameras were rolling, capturing every shot and slam dunk. We were so close to the court that we could see the sweat spraying off the players, occasionally landing just inches from our feet. Then all of a sudden, my phone rang and vibrated, I looked down to see, it was my son. I picked up the phone urgently, and as I said hello, he asked, "Where are you?" his voice filled with curiosity. "I'm in Mami for a meeting and will be home in the morning," I shared. He pressed on, "No, but where are you right now?" I answered, "In Miami, my son," as I told him again. With a pause, he then started laughing, "Okay, well, I just saw you on TV" "You're at the Heat and Bulls game, how can that be?" The camera had zoomed in our us several times, my new friend from Florida and me. The game was fantastic and I made it home with a good memory from that day.

Lesson learned:

You are always being observed. Every movement and every sound being recorded. Actions will continue to be studied with each passing day. Long before children can do anything else, they learn to watch. For me, I was learning that my most important audience was my kids.

Chapter 24

2014 Sideswiped in Mexico

With the kids away for a week, I decided it was time to return to my sanctuary, time to head back to home, Mexico, that is. This was where I wanted to be, a more laid-back vibe and serene solitude that only this place could offer. It was a place where our family would escape the chaos and stress of everyday life, though I knew better than to believe you could truly run from your problems. Still, a little time away can do wonders for the soul. This trip, I had a thrilling twist in mind, I invited an old work colleague, a crush from out West to join me. We planned to meet in Puerto Vallarta, where we'd then head straight to the beach. I was looking forward to soaking up some sunshine and relaxing by the bay, but there was an electric undercurrent to my anticipation, I couldn't help but wonder if this getaway might ignite something more between us, perhaps turning our old friendship into a tantalizing new chapter. I would test the waters to see if this friendship was something more.

Soaring through customs, I knew my way well, walking past family vacationers as they were bombarded by offers of special deals at this place. Taxis and shuttle drivers zeroed in on their prey as they left me alone as I knew the game. Their efforts were fruitless. My head was covered with my Yankees baseball cap and sunglasses on tight. Most knew who I was, they knew me by face. A seasoned gringo in Mexico, they left me alone. I moved through the crowds and across the street, over to the parking lot as I always arranged. My truck sat waiting for me, parked in its spot. With keys under the mat, I was ready to go.

My friend from Phoenix had not yet arrived, so I drove into Puerto Vallarta to load up on supplies. The driving here is different than in the U.S. You better know the law as these cops play for keeps. Simple things such as turning left, one must follow the rules. You want to turn left, then get to the right. Gringos from "Gringolandia" can't come here to set the pace. I see it all the time. When you are a foreigner, a visitor, for sure, follow the rules and respect the culture. Respect the people, respect the land, and embrace the differences. This paradise is a beautiful place.

Loaded up with tequila, ice-cold cervezas, and fresh local treats, I was ready to go. Back to the airport I roared to pick up my friend. The traffic was crazy this time of the year. My truck moved slowly through the traffic jam and towards the line of people waiting with suitcases and golf clubs, itching to get out of their winter gear for some sun and sand. There were more people wanting to come to this oasis than the airport could handle.

As I rounded the corner, I could see my friend curbside. Should I give her a hug, or shake her hand? I didn't know what to do. I pulled to the side and got out of the truck. Greeted her with excitement and gave her a kiss, I didn't have a clue. My emotional intuition told me that didn't feel right, but I was yearning for romance once again. This was my friend, my old work buddy, and here I was trying to change the mood. The drive down the beach was great as we reconnected. I had missed our good times of working and laughing together. As the road opened up with our windows down, I hit the gas as the ocean breeze came across us, I was losing focus fast. I was soon reminded of my driving skills as I saw flashing blue lights coming up behind us fast. Damn, I thought, a few days in the sun with my friend and already getting pulled over within a few hours of landing. I had to act fast. I grabbed my wallet quickly and looked at the cash, pulling some out, I kept it in hand. Una policia vestido de azul, I knew the drill. "Licencia y registro por favor" he said. He shared that this was a problem and would take the rest of the day. I knew that was bullshit but I had to play. So, I asked him politely if I could give him the pesos to pay for my fine, a favor he would be doing so we could be on our way. After 10 minutes or more we had reached an agreement. I gave him the dinero and he committed to pay. One drama diverted as we got to the casa and unpacked for a few days. It was great being together, though we both really knew we were just going to remain friends. That's all we could do. To cross that line ever would have destroyed what we had. We tested the water a few more times, and both agreed without words that what we had was more like a brother-sister relationship to leave as it was. Things were going great now as we got that out of the way.

We decided to drive back into Puerto Vallarta for a little excitement the following day. The Malecon was buzzing as a cruise ship had just come into port. More gringos had docked now and were ready to play, with excitement and energy, they flooded the town but in a good way. Tourist dollars are important as it helps keep the economy afloat.

Speaking of Puerto Vallarta, let me share with you some background and interesting facts as part of my story. While many look to go to this coastal area for the beaches and fun in the sun, Puerto Vallarta is also rich in history as the town dates back to the mid-1800s. Known initially as Puerto Las Penas in 1851, the name was changed in 1918. The city of Puerto Vallarta is the government seat of the Municipality of Puerto Vallarta and is located in the state of Jalisco. The town grew rapidly with the establishment of banana plantations in the area since the 20's and despite a history of hurricanes, it continues to grow in popularity. Unique to this town, it is protected to some extent from direct

174

hits off the Pacific Ocean due to its location in Banderas Bay. The bay offers some protection as it is approximately 60 some miles long and 26 miles across, with a depth of up to 3,000 feet, making it a natural breeding ground for humpback whales to come from November thru April to mate and give birth. In town, the Church of Our Lady of Guadalupe, locally known as Iglesia de Nuestra Senora de Guadalupe, is a site to see. A Catholic place of worship, it is distinguished by its neoclassical building style in the main chapel and renaissance-style towers above. If you are not set on having your sins being forgiven, the town has an abundance of nightlife with bars and clubs. To satisfy your hunger, I'd estimate there to be close to 1,000 restaurants within the area, with choices to satisfy any pallet. The town was also put on the map with the filming of a number of movies, some of which you may be familiar with: Revenge, Predator, and Limitless, to name a few. The most famous of movie originally filmed here was Night of the Iguana, directed by none other than John Huston, who had a love for this place. The streets of Vallarta also became a celebrity hotspot and city known for romance, with the news of a love affair between Elizabeth Taylor and Richard Burton just a year before the filming of this movie in 1963.

While it was clear that a love affair was not in the air for my friend and I, we did have a good time as we drank, ate, and laughed together that day. After a few more hours of fun, I was ready to get us back to the beach. Through the big city and past the airport, we navigated our way home.

Back to the beach town, we were 15 minutes away. We decided to pull off to stop at the Mega, a supermarket, for some beverages as we were going right by. If you have driven around the bay and outskirts around Puerto Vallarta, you know that alongside the main road, there also is a side service road that follows at times. This road is typically used for getting on and exiting off the main road with various "openings" throughout. Remember, in Mexico, if you want to turn left, you need to get off to the right. Also, in many cases, the two roads are divided by beautiful rows of tall Bougainvillea flowering plants that hide what is on the other side.

So, off to the side and onto the service road I steered. At the same time, a girl, a young lady, I would say, was motoring her scooter down the service road along the other side of these beautiful rows of gorgeous pinkish-red pedal plants. Our timing was perfect, with her at full throttle as I veered off the main road. Her front wheel connected with my back right side. She went down hard and tumbled and spilled. At over 40 miles per hour, her scooter flew into pieces as she skidded and slid down the asphalt. My mind raced with options at that moment in a flash. Do I keep going? Hell no, I needed to stop and help this girl out. I thought of my daughter, what would I do. We pulled over to the side and ran to her rescue. Her jeans and shirt were torn apart; thank God she had a helmet. In the middle of the road, I sat and held her head in my lap. She was bloody and torn up as we called for some help. Within minutes the police and then ambulance arrived. I was grilled hard by the cops as they wanted to place blame on the Gringo, I'd be the guy. First things first, I wanted to make sure this girl was going to be ok. While she was cut up and bruised, there were no broken bones from what I could see. She was given first aid, and then, to be sure, the ambulance raced her to the hospital for X-rays, she was going to be fine. During this time, her father and brother were called to the scene. So here it was, 4 cops, the father, the brother, my friend, and me.

For 3 hours in the scolding heat on the side of the

road, I was grilled hard like a criminal. The heat was intense in more than one way. Sweat pouring down off my face, these guys would not relent. They screamed at me in Spanish for me to acknowledge my sin for hitting this poor girl and to sign a confession, I would most likely go to jail. I held my ground and tried as best I could to reason in Spanish, but these guys would not back down. I shared photos on my phone I had taken of the placement of the truck and scooter, and it was obvious to see, it was pure bad timing and no one to blame. As I had serious contacts in the bay, I called on these local power players who helped me right then. They came to my rescue and talked these cops down. Some cash was paid out to settle the situation, along with pesos to cover all medical bills, I even fronted the dinero to buy a new scooter. All was going to be well. The deal was agreed to, and handshakes were made. Then, all of a sudden, our conversation shifted to English. I was a little surprised. The father and brother offered some water for us, and the policias locales gave me high fives. We were all friends now and this was a thing of the past, as new relationships were forged. It's important to note that you need to make friends in this country, not enemies, to fight.

Shaken emotionally and physically tired, we made it back to the house with a new story to tell. I was hoping for no more drama but life just wouldn't stay still.

Lesson learned:

Keep your eyes focused on the road and both of your hands tight on the wheel. You never know when you might hit a slick spot, face a sudden roadblock, or encounter a blind spot that's impossible to see. Life's a wild ride and distractions can strike when you're speeding or moving slow. It can happen out of nowhere when you are not looking and knock you down fast. This business of living can sometimes be hard, and while the journey barrels onward, I remind myself to keep learning, keep growing, and keep moving forward.

Chapter 25

2017 Grand Jury Ain't That Grand

A few more years rolled by with their fair share of surprises and challenges. Just like everyone else, my life danced between highs and lows. Amid juggling work, kids and family chaos, I kept chasing the elusive spark of romance, though true love seemed as distant as ever.

One evening, as I drifted through my monotonous one-hour commute back home, my mind was on autopilot, a zombie navigating the familiar grind. I pulled into the driveway where more routine awaited me: parking the car, dragging the garbage cans into the garage, and shuffling to the mailbox. Inside, a mundane collection of bills and junk mail awaited. Monthly statements mixed in with ads and offers, a call for fleeting pleasures and distractions, tempting me to seek happiness in material things. Like a deadly drug, a short-term fix for happiness for many. Yet, I learned to resist. My life had settled into a quiet rhythm, simple and unadorned, as I embraced the peace within plainness.

As I scanned through the mail, I saw an official letter. Was it junk mail or something of importance. These marketers were good at catching your eye. I opened it up and read what was inside. It was a summons of sorts, something I had never seen before, like in the movies or on the news from what I could tell. I read it again and again and it sounded legit. I checked out the website, and it was for real. I was called in for jury duty. Not the type you might be familiar with, this was a bigger event, it was a grand deal. I was being called up for the Federal Grand Jury. What the hell!

This Federal Grand Jury thing is really something. Try as hard as you can it's tough to get out of. You better be dying or have a great hardship. Once confirmed that you have been one of the chosen few, you better be ready as your life now includes sitting behind closed doors 3 full days per month between 12 - 18 months. No laptops or phones, you are working, my friends, as this in itself becomes quite a unique journey.

Let me share with you some facts about a Federal Grand Jury. If you are one of the select few, that puts you in about .03% +/- of the adult population that gets called on to be part of this group. A grand jury will determine to bring charges against a suspect or to hand down an indictment triggering a criminal case. To add to the mystery and increase the drama, a grand jury is private and prohibits most persons from disclosing any details of a case. With a pay of $20 per day, it'll just about cover your daily lunch.

Compare that to regular jury duty and the odds raise to around 27% you are sent a notice to serve. If you have ever been called for regular jury service, then you know that you show up to a courthouse and wait to be summoned. If your number comes up then you do your duty and help to decide guilt or innocence as you render a verdict. If it doesn't get called, you are done, and you get to go home.

I did my grand jury time and it was painful, no doubt.

If you travel for work or work after hours, then you better prepare for your life to get thrown off as you do this service. What I do have to say is that you do get to hear the extraordinary of cases, from gangsters to drug rings, corporate fraud and planned-out murders.

Lesson learned:

I walked away smarter in an unanticipated way learning better to be fair and impartial using facts without feelings or using emotion.

Chapter 26

2019 Wild Rides

If not you, then who? If not now, then when? (A version of a comment with origins that lies with a guy by the name of Hillel, the Elder if you are interested to know.)

It has been said, and I do agree that there is never a perfect time to start a business, so why not start today. If you wait until you are ready, you will be waiting for the rest of your life. My oldest son, just a spry twenty-something at the time, was itching to turn his car obsession into a full-blown business, looking to turn his dream into a reality. His passion for European cars was something that we both reveled in, bonding over every sleek curve and engine purr was pure satisfaction. This passion and a love and appreciation specifically for European cars was something that I also shared as it helped to create a natural father son bond. Eager to help him fuel his dreams, I jumped into kickstart to help him get things rolling.

It's one thing to have big ideas and wild dreams, but turning them into reality demands action, discipline and a sense of urgency to make things happen, traits to be learned that separate the players from the watchers, the dreamers from the doers. That was a lesson I was determined to impart and to teach him along the way. What we didn't see coming was the COVID-19 storm that slammed into us in early 2020, grinding everything to a screeching halt.

Two years ago, he was helping to grow a startup used car business with a friend he knew well. This "friend," we will say, gave an offer to my son, the worker bee and all-around hustler, who would take the reins and run the show with a promise of a juicy slice of the profits. The offer was made and they were now working together. A handshake was used to cement the deal as this young kid, my son, thought a promise is a promise. They did the right things to make the business grow, from a great street location and an improved website for sales. At their peak they had sold over 200 cars in one year just these two. As the money rolled in, so did the broken promises. The deal had been broken as no ownership was shared, so this young kid decided to go out on his own. He learned a good lesson about business that year: Work hard, be smart but you better beware. There are "lemons" and dishonesty wherever you go. Make sure you align with people with ethics and people you can trust. As he learned through this process, a handshake by some means nothing at all. Get your agreement in writing to make sure it's for real.

I give this kid credit as he wasn't defeated. He searched for a new location in another state. Across the river, he decided to go. A cool building, an old warehouse, large enough for freight cars is what he had found. He located the owner and struck a deal for this place. A small old man was the landlord here. His passion for old cars seemed to make this a good fit. He had an interesting history with a mystery and allure. A frail man of structure, he seemed innocent of a kind. What we didn't know at the time was that underneath the hood of that old soul was what I considered to be a menacing plotter looking to offer what was now thought of as just foul gold.

A contract was drafted for this new business venture. My son, the main owner, the old man and myself, the investor, almost played for a fool. Full throttle we went to get this business up and running while the storm called COVID-19 was brewing eight months away before this epidemic would land at the doorstep.

The kid got the dealer license secured and a work use permit approved by the city and village. We were told he was now the youngest known person to have a car dealership in the state. What an accomplishment he had made to keep things rolling. For me I was proud as I watched this unfold. I threw money at it like crazy to build out the site. Electrical and plumbing and serious cleanup were needed.

The old man had some friends, and workers that he had hired to offer their help. A crackhead mechanic and a meth addict fugitive on the run. A sketchy crew we now had though we let it go. These two helpers were living incognito in this old warehouse, if you can believe it. The plot was thickening, and soon, this wasn't much fun. These two

187

characters with the old man were now acting together, a trio on the darker side, that was for sure. We had been sucked in badly as they worked on us hard. Their agenda was much different than ours. This was no partnership, it appeared to be a scam. Doing dishonest work and grabbing money wherever they could. They worked every angle, not like partners should do. In spite of their behavior, with the doors finally opened, sales started to trickle in. Mercedes, BMWs, Rovers and Jags started to cover the floor. Even Mini Coopers and Audis were now offered on stage. While we did our best to monitor the greasing hands of this new crew, we didn't anticipate what was coming as it was now heading our way.

At the end of the year, as 2020 drew near, COVID-19 hit like a sledgehammer, and within a matter of months, the business had to be closed. Lots of hard work, sweat and money poured into it seemed to evaporate with little to show. This once bustling warehouse now stood vacant, a stark reminder of dreams interrupted. But amidst the rubble, invaluable lessons emerged. The journey of turning a vision into reality proved to be an education in itself and was one lesson of a few, something never to be learned in a classroom. Navigating the labyrinth of city council meetings, inspections, and complex business contracts was like earning a PhD in real-world entrepreneurship. This experience was more intense than any top business school could provide; it was learned on the streets and forged in the fire. It was a hands-on crash course in resilience and adaptability, one that will serve as a guiding light for future ventures.

Lesson learned:

Amidst the struggles and setbacks, profound lessons often reveal themselves, not just for the one who endures but sometimes for those who witness the journey. I watched my son navigate a mountain of challenges: grabbling with thugs, wrestling with bureaucratic red tape, and surmounting unforeseen obstacles. Through hardship and adversity, there can be a true treasure to be found. While he may not know it, the time I spent alongside him was my priceless reward.

Chapter 27

2021 Hookers & Blow & Things I Didn't Know

After COVID-19 had me feeling utterly depleted, I decided it was time for a change of scenery with a move outside of the U.S. My kids were all older now and doing their own thing, so I headed back to the beach, where I could work remotely and soak up some sunshine in a place that made me feel at ease. After a little travel across the U.S. and throughout Latin America, I now used Mexico as my home base.

The next 12-18 months proved to be a whirlwind of physical challenges as many will endure. First up was a struggle with a motility disorder, specifically an esophageal stricture. Imagine trying to eat but having the food get stuck, leading to choking and barfing. It felt like being waterboarded with food instead of water, an excruciating ordeal. It's a painful experience that can be fixed relatively fast. Shove a balloon down your throat and pump it up full; it stretches your esophagus, and then it's all better.

My eyes were the next thing that started to go. For nearly two years, my sight was beginning to deteriorate fast. Gazing out at the horizon became a distant memory and was a thing of the past. Seeing at night was a feat in itself. Every light became a starburst, distorting my view as if I were driving at night through a storm of fiery red-hot embers blowing across the sky. Try playing a sport while balls seem to vanish in mid-air. Thankfully, cataract surgery was a game changer. With my vision restored, it granted me a fresh perspective on life, transforming more than just my sight, though it would still take time to see things clearly.

While now working in Mexico, I found myself with unexpected free time, which led me to dive headfirst into the

191

local community. A novelty no more, I soon became an accepted part of this vibrant beach town. I made it my mission to forge connections and lend a hand wherever it was needed. Making friends and helping others was what I started to do. I quietly wove myself into the fabric of the community, discovering the rich tapestry of life in a place that had quickly become my home.

With one of my very good friends visiting me from the states, though COVID-19 was present, we used this time to enjoy the libations of the many local drinking establishments in this quiet fishing village. It was easy to do as being in a tropical paradise we spent most of our time outdoors. A few days into his visit, I was sitting at a table out front of a restaurant, waiting as he was getting his haircut at La Barberia. Fate struck me hard without any warning. I was on the phone doing business as a goddess appeared. On the dusty streets, she walked past me with her two kids by her side and right then and there, I was hooked…line and sinker. I dropped my phone from my face and hung up real fast as they sat down at a table across from me. The dopamine surged throughout my body. I felt a sense of temporary pleasure like nothing before, thinking this is how heroin or ecstasy must make you feel. This tingling in my body was something even more. Endorphins of happiness were a hormone I think I now had. Maybe even some serotonin was in the mix. Could it be this longer lasting feeling of well-being was now within reach?

This Canadian, Italian hottie by descent, was beautiful both inside and out from what I could tell. With mystery and intrigue, I was all in for this action. From Canada to Columbia: Cali and Bogota, Belize and then Mexico, she had fled with her children from some danger of the past. I felt a sense of chivalry as I could help, I'd be the man of the hour and save them from suffering. Little did I know that this new journey was going to be a ride like no other.

The courtship went fast as the chemistry was strong. A mix of insane partying and other crazy stuff, this combination was toxic and probably not made to last. With rock star-like sex anyplace, anywhere, we did it all. Within a few months, she had moved in with me as I became her savior and, looking back, her for me. We both gave each other something that we each needed. To each other, we filled the void of something we didn't have. She loved her kids dearly and they had a special connection with her too. She really did try to keep everything stable, but the pressure kept mounting no matter what she would do. To help with the education, she had arranged for a private school for these boys, and now, with a safe place to stay, I was hoping things would settle down.

I loved this woman as we had a connection like no other. Playing cards on the deck overlooking the bay, we would talk, drink red wine, her smoking her cigs and me with my Cubans. We understood each other's background and went deep into each other's psychics as our feelings continued to grow. As she tried to run from her past, the shadow kept lurking and just wouldn't go away. As hard as she tried to move forward, it was too much to handle. For me, my fix or my high was in trying to help. Like a powerful drug such as morphine or oxycodone, we relied on each other to help both mask our pain. We were addicted to each other, but not in a good way. However, our love was real, it was deep and would never go away.

Next came some more health issues, which was a major surprise. Lots of testing, poking and prodding and then the news I had feared. I had prostate cancer that was aggressively growing. One tumor was found, and then I had two, so now I was in a position where I had to decide what to do. Thank God it had not metastasized or moved into other parts of my body, or this story would have been over that day. When you share you have prostate cancer, it's interesting to hear some people say, "At least it's only prostate cancer." I always thought that was an odd or weird way to comfort people in that situation. "It's only...blah blah blah," like it's not a big deal. I elected to have radical robotic surgery, and it was the right thing to do as, to date, the cancer is out of my body, and I'm feeling quite well. The short-term effects can be painful I can tell you that for sure. The feeling of being emasculated or having your machismo taken from you is a hit to the soul. The good news is after a year or two the feeling came back. "God, thank you!" I said to myself more days than one. My lover, best friend, now she was a champ. She took care of me through all this and I was blessed for that.

Deeper and deeper, our relationship grew, though it was turning into something that was bad for us all. As the days went on, she couldn't break away from her troubled past. Her problems became our crusade together as this was now our bond. During this time our circle of connections went deeper as well. Underground, we went into this Mexican bay. We knew most of the drug dealers and how to get around. From the players to punks, we knew them all. The homeless and wealthy business owners and even hookers we knew. The families and tienda store owners, we were part of their lives.

We built strong relations at every possible level. From the dudes on the streets to the offices on the hill, we were protected by the locals no matter our situation as our drama continued and grew. This magical town protected their people and we did the same whenever we could. For the locals in general, we tried to be good to them all. The schools and the orphanages we supported them well and my soul mate, my love, would help others in her very special way. Giving to others who had nothing at all, it's something not many knew of her from her look and her way. But there was a kindness deep in her troubled heart. Sadly, the demons within her wouldn't leave her as hard as she tried. Regardless, we forged onward together to try to make this life right.

Lesson learned:

Love is something you create and sometimes something you find. On other occasions, this beautiful gift may even find you. Sadly, I hadn't quite learned that love is not always enough.

Chapter 28

2022 Snortin' Tequilla &

Drinkin' Cocaine

Our saga continued as our presence in both the US and Mexico began to stir curiosity and intrigue. Wherever we went, heads turned, whispers filled the air: "Who are these people?" they would all say. They wondered if we were formidable figures, shadowy operatives, or simply ambitious dreamers, just wannabes. We were cruising in sleek Mercedes and rugged Rovers, living the high life with properties in Mexico and the US. Our mobility was unmatched, allowing us to navigate our dual worlds with ease. Our transformation was subtle, almost imperceptible at times, but it was undeniable, we were turning into something different as you can see. A slow transformation it's easy to miss when it's happening to you.

Back in Mexico, we craved more privacy and wanted to blend seamlessly into the local culture, so we embarked on a quest for land where we could build our sanctuary amidst the community, not in some upscale, expatriate enclave. We sought authenticity, a place where we would be embraced and accepted by the locals, where we knew there was a way better fit. We looked long and hard and found the perfect spot. A rare gem of a property, nearly a quarter of a city block. This was land you could only get by knowing the right people and through insider connections and not found on any realtor website. It was exactly what we needed and fit us perfectly for what we were trying to do. Previously owned by a local family that was handed down by generations from years of the past, the deal came together smoothly thanks to our local connections. The contacts we had made from living here now had proved useful as we weren't jerked around. With the help of a trusted Notario, the paperwork and transaction were completed swiftly, with no realtor or go-between, this happened fast. It was a straightforward deal, ensuring that everyone came out ahead. The property was ours and our next chapter in Mexico was ready to unfold.

Our vision for the casa was nothing short of a secluded sanctuary, with its tall adobe walls and terracotta roof tiles giving nothing away from the street. Inside, we planned for a hacienda ranch-style retreat blended seamlessly with a tropical flair. Walking inside with airy living rooms with sunken floors flowing throughout aside from a grand courtyard with an impressive-sized pool. Our architect, a true artist dived into our dream with unparalleled dedication and went hard to work. He listened to our desires and drew up the plans, and hit the mark right down to the wrought iron fixtures, artisanal tilework and hand-carved wooden doors. The site was cleared and ready to go. The soil and water testing came back with a green light to go, with no issues at all, so the city gave us our approval to start building this estate. We were set to start construction and move into this magnificent dream home the following year.

Meanwhile, my life became a bit of a whirlwind of travel again as I bounced between Mexico, the U.S. and Europe for work, wherever I was required to be, as my gal remained in Mexico with her kids while they attended school. It was a temporary arrangement as the months passed and worked for a while, but it was growing old fast. The strain of constant separation began to wear on us now. Unbeknownst to me, while I was away, she was battling her own demons, shadows from her past that clung to her in my absence and was eroding her mind and would not leave her alone. During the kid's school vacations, we tried to reconnect, traveling together to various places. While we stayed in beautiful Banderas Bay most of the time, she did take her kids to Canada to see relatives and cousins for various family gatherings. We even made it back to the U.S. for a little fun. Despite all the challenges, we continued to chase moments of joy amidst all the chaos.

Our partying was hard-core and was getting even more intense. The booze we threw down fast and the stuff on the table was a real treat. When the kids were not with us, we would go out for dinners and dance at open-air venues where live local bands set the stage. Wherever we went, these places knew us well the moment we entered; the entire atmosphere shifted. Diners and drinkers alike felt the electric charge of our presence. One night, during a sultry Mexican tune, we drew every eye on us as we stepped onto the dance floor. The song was an intoxicating blend of sensual salsa and passionate Argentine tango. It was seductive and sexy, and the crowd was in awe. It's hard to describe that moment that night as we danced slowly together, our bodies as one, entwined in a slow, rhythmic embrace. With my hands slowly gliding through her long, wavy hair, our every twist and turn became a display of grace and intensity. It was sexual and breathtaking on that dance floor that night. The people in the restaurant and the bar, they all fell into a trance as they stood there watching in silence, fully mesmerized during that time. The song's final notes lingered softly as it was coming to an end. As reality set back in, the crowd broke into applause, rushing over to us, sharing that it was the most captivating, hot, romantic dance they'd ever seen.

Our lives were a captivating paradox. No matter how hard people tried, no one could figure us out. By day, we sculpted our physiques with rigorous workouts: crazy aerobics, swimming and weights to keep our bodies hard and lean. By night, we indulged in wild parties and carousing of every kind. We could appear scruffy and disheveled one moment yet effortlessly splurge on vehicles and land the next. At times, we looked homeless but we had tons of cash, and her kids started to thrive in private school as they were now settling in.

We were still living hard and continued to push life to the edge. Sadly, my love's problems just wouldn't go away. Threats from afar you can't imagine, pushed her deeper and deeper where she just couldn't break free. Her mind and her soul were in a permanent prison, she could never get out. The darkness around her started staying longer and longer and just won't leave. At times, she would go into a psychosis that was painful to watch. At one point, she had disappeared for a few days, supposedly roaming the streets, not knowing where she was. It wasn't her fault as the demons took over. A traumatic event with many involved, the kids ended up in Mexico City with the dad and they were now nowhere to be found. It sadly just happened as the battle raged on. These kids, in the middle of a terrible war, had disappeared for good now, they were completely gone. Not sure of which borough or alcaldias they were in, it was impossible to tell of which neighborhood they lived. We had heard the kids were in a school as the dad tried his best while my love started working with attorneys to try to gain access to her children in any possible way. These kids were being pulled in every direction, and I was thinking they didn't have a chance. An endless fight for these youngsters, it was killing us all and changing this woman, she was giving up slowly.

Working with Canadian, U.S. and Mexican Embassies and multiple attorneys, too, it had now become an international affair. Back and forth from Mexico to the U.S., we would go and on occasion, she would go to Canada as well, working with government officials trying to help with no avail. With all the multiple trips and traveling, we ended up on a short list, it appeared. Our names and faces were now being watched while our itineraries, I believe, were also being tracked. On one trip in particular we were stopped in Minnesota before entering the jetway in front of a crowd. I was grabbed by a guy in a Carhartt Detroit Duck jacket, wearing work boots, quite plain, and my gal stopped by a lady wearing a hoodie and jeans. These people were undercover, and they questioned us hard. Our story was real with paperwork to support us, so with the final boarding call, we were allowed to get on the plane. We were the last travelers to sit down with everyone to see.

Whatever the reasons, I just couldn't break free of this drama that continued to plague me, it just wouldn't leave. Days and some weeks were spent in Mexico City fighting in court. The judicial system and bureaucracy are so large, a nightmare to say the least. Like a maze spread across multiple countries with no exit in sight. Round after round, it was an unending battle, like being in the middle of a pelea de gallos Mexicana with no winner, just losers ultimately, from what I could see. All during this time, her will to live continued to fade.

I needed a break from this nonstop soap opera, and she went back to Canada as I tried to decide what I should do. She lived with some of her friends and worked odd jobs throughout. Working on ranches and resorts, to name just a few. She worked hard to save money to pay for attorneys to help get her kids. Now back to Mexico City, she went with cash in her pocket she got taken badly by some smooth operators. All her hard work to help find her children was gone in a flash. This time, it nearly killed her, but she continued to fight. Then, from Mexico to New York now, she stayed for a while as she made a few friends, I'm not sure how that came about. I could see the pages in her chapters kept turning towards the end.

We talked through the issues and after her being in New York for some partying over New Year's, I picked her up to try this again. To mask our core problems and pain, I leaned in on what I knew best, a business for us to start, a new common goal. We focused on a plan that had been a vision for some time: to provide convenience throughout the Mexican Bay. This business was soon unfolding to offer an online ordering and delivery service. It was brilliant and needed, as we had found a unique niche where people were willing to pay. To add to the drama, we threw a marriage into the mix as our lives just continued to get more complex.

Lesson learned:

I was close to seeing but hadn't learned quite yet, that walking away was as important as what I walked toward. I had to listen to the sound of my feet walking away from things not meant for me. I just hadn't taken that first step.

Chapter 29

2023 Gone Forever

I refused to give up no matter the odds and now here we were back together in the upper Mid-West. Together in the dead of winter near the Canadian border, we stayed. We needed a break from all of mankind, so we hibernated away for a few months on our own. The hideaway is where we decided to stay. A log house with a fireplace, we tried to chill out. Wherever we went, people wanted to know, who are these two characters that didn't belong here. We yearned for some privacy but it was impossible to attain.

Then, one day, we openly greeted a new guest. A dog, a beautiful creature, had come to our door. Like magic from heaven, a connection was made. This gentle malamute came here to deliver a message, I believe. We learned his name was Nanook, the Inuit name for a polar bear, known as the greatest hunting animal of the north. Known to be aggressive but stealthy and a spiritual ideal, Nanooks polar bears are the ultimate masters in the snow. The Inuit hunters would worship these great beasts as they believed that these animals decided if hunters deserved success. Nanook, our new dog calmed us with comfort with his presence worthy of great respect. He would appear like the wind out of nowhere and would stay with us for days, then be gone just as quietly, he would disappear. There was more to this than coincidence, I firmly believe, a spirit that was needed during this time while we were here.

With time on our hands being up in the north, we built out our Mexico delivery business, a killer website and people to support it. We were ready to launch at the end of the year when the crowds came back to the beaches, our team would be fulfilling orders right to their doors. We were set on this business to take us to the next level.

Our next stop was Vegas but not for play. I still had some security business to do. At the same time, we planned on taking that next matrimonial step. True to our personalities and to cement our special bond, we made plans to take the plunge. We headed over to Clark County to file the papers. Then, a few days later, to Elvis Presley's wedding chapel, we would go. We said our "I dos," and it was now official.

From Vegas back up North to the hideaway we went for a while. We spent the spring and summer up there as things really unraveled. The battle in Mexico was becoming a great loss, and the memories of her children left open scares that wouldn't go away. She went deeper and deeper into the abyss of a living hell on this earth and there was no way for me to help, nothing I could do or nothing I could say. There was no getting out of this deep state she was in. Our drama exploded and our life became a mess. The pressure of it all mixed in with our love became toxic as we tried as hard as we could to work at it together. With some counseling and course correction we thought that might help. It was finally late Fall now, and we had a plan, we were ready to go.

Back in Mexico, we went to get back to our home. We yearned for the beach with sunrises and sunsets, this was our place of peace where we belonged. Launching the business and our friends by our side, we hoped this would do it and get us back to a more common stride. We came in back soft but it all started over. The drama and stress grew worse than before. Within weeks, the dusty side streets took over my love as the demons of the past pulled her back fast. I don't even know if she knew where she was as she roamed through the town in a daze, in a complete trance. It was too much for anyone to handle this type of emotional pain as the memories all came rolling back. With her children away, though alive somewhere, this was a pain that no parent should have to endure. I was helpless in helping her and was losing the battle. I lost my wife as we lost each other. Worse of it all, she ended up losing herself as there was nothing more she could handle.

Lesson learned:

Choose to be hopeful in the midst of it all. Challenges in life will follow wherever you go. I realized my help in helping her wasn't helping anymore. My pain that was growing came from my inability to stop someone from dying. I needed to practice acceptance and compassion while letting things go.

Chapter 30
2024 There's No Place Like Home

I had enough, no more could I take. I tried so hard but this life was taking me down. On my own, I packed my bags and went back to the U.S., to the hideaway I went to figure things out. My eyesight was pretty clear now, and I started to see that this whole thing was killing me. I needed to help myself and heal from the years of the past. A lot of reflection and thinking about how to move forward.

Forgiveness to myself and sharing kindness, and being compassionate to others, that's what I'm trying to do.

At one time, I heard she was still on those dusty Mexican streets looking for her children deep in her mind. It is the saddest of things that anyone could bear, the pain and suffering that comes from within. I wish for her some peace however that can be found. At one point I heard she had traveled to Los Angeles with help from a friend, people all trying to help her in any way they could. Then, more rumors of her going back to Mexico and up to Canada for a while. I'm really not sure if she is dead or alive. As that's the last I heard of her as this story now comes to an end.

While this story may be done, the journey is far from over. What I can tell you now and as you may know, it's been one hell of a road trip and one hell of a ride. Airplanes, autos, a few wives in the mix, and mystery and intrigue while traveling and working in over 45 countries during this time. I'd never trade my life for anything less. My promise to myself is to continue to learn from my experiences and actions. With eyes wide open, I know there is a lot more that I can do, as one thing is for certain: growth and learning should never stop. It's a journey that continues till our last breath and beyond. With self-reflection, empathy, gratitude and more, I want to leave goodwill toward others wherever I go.

Lesson learned:

In the blink of one eye, another day will pass by. Another week, another month, and they're gone just as well. Then comes a year as they all disappear. In the blink of another eye, we'll all be gone too. So maybe, just maybe, we should be taking a breath and look at the moment and the road we are on. Appreciate it, love it and see where it goes. Don't fight it, embrace it, but make corrections along the way. You see, we all have a story that we can tell. It's never too late wherever you are, keep your eyes wide open, moving forward each day and try to do the best you can do, that is all I will say.

About the Author

E.J. Rosenwinkel spends his time in solitude now going back and forth from "the hideaway", a few hours from the Canadian border to a now "not so sleepy" beach town near Puerto Vallarta, Mexico, both of which where he and his last, loved, lost wife, attempted to avoid drama amidst a global backdrop and on this magnificent stage called life.

Made in the USA
Coppell, TX
16 October 2024

38726571R00122